MW00888473

GROW A PEAR

A Guide to Improved Emotional Intelligence

Michael Cornwall PsyD PhD

ISBN: 9781073125142

Illustrations by Patience Camille Forbes

This book is dedicated to Albert Ellis, Glenn Deason, and the King of the First Grade.

Table of Contents

WELCOME

Emotional Intelligence (EI) refers to the ability to recognize and understand one's emotions, as well as the feelings of others, and to use this awareness to manage emotional behavior. Optimal EI is the ability to perceive, express, understand, and regulate emotions in a way that is more likely to produce adaptive results. EI is important because it helps us communicate effectively, build strong relationships, and make better decisions. EI also plays a role in conflict resolution, generic problem-solving, and personal well-being. Several critical skills and competencies are associated with improved EI:

- *Self-awareness* or the ability to recognize and understand one's own emotions and their impact on others;
- *Self-regulation* or the ability to manage one's own emotions and behaviors;
- *Motivation* or the ability to use one's emotions to drive and achieve goals;
- *Empathy* or the ability to understand and respond to the feelings of others;
- *Social skills* or the ability to effectively communicate and build relationships with others.

Some people are naturally more emotionally intelligent than others, but emotional intelligence can be developed and improved through training and practice. This manuscript offers skills that can improve EI for anyone, regardless of their present skill level.

SOME BACKGROUND ON EI

Theorists have adapted EI as a form of psychotherapy that recognizes biological, psychological, and social learning (biopsychosocial) as essential to constructing and expressing adaptive emotion. The biopsychosocial influence on emotional health trusts the notion that an individual's physical and mental health can be affected by both biological and environmental factors.

Biological factors include an individual's genetics, epigenetics, natural development, and biological rhythms. Environmental influences include a person's lifestyle, diet, stress level, social interaction, and access to resources. Psychological factors include each of these components, as well as individual thinking, perception, and learned behaviors. These elements are interconnected and can overlap to create a complex web of influence on emotional expression.

Michael Cornwall

One of the more well-known proponents of the biopsychosocial model was Albert Ellis (September 27, 1913–July 24, 2007), an American psychologist who developed Rational Emotive Behavior Therapy (REBT). As a theory of emotional management, Ellis endorsed a whole-person approach to psychological health. Ellis' REBT recognized the influence of cognitive restructuring on stress management, helping to mediate the body's response to life's challenges through better thought and body management.

REBT's central premise is the ABC Model, which suggests that our emotional responses to events are affected by our beliefs about events and not the events themselves. The theory proposes that we can first gain insight into our physical and emotional reactions to experiences by first managing the body and its response to thought, followed by challenging the ideas, perceptions, and meaning we place on events.

George L. Engel and Jon Romano discussed biopsychosocial theory in 1977 in their paper *The Need for a New Medical Model: A Challenge for Biomedicine*. Engel and Romano emphasized that biological and social factors can profoundly impact emotional expression and global well-being. Their ideas recognize the bond between the mind and the body and provide a model for achieving comprehensive physical and emotional wellness.

Peter Salovey and John D. Mayer proposed their ideas on EI in 1990 in their paper entitled *Emotional Intelligence*, defining it as the ability to monitor thoughts and behaviors. The key to improved EI, they believed, relied on using less stringent, more flexible, fair, and tolerant beliefs for ourselves and others. They suggested that improvement in EI was possible if we learned to think more rationally by choosing:

1. Truth over fiction
2. Courage over inaction
3. Leadership by example
4. Individuality
5. Resilience
6. Composure
7. Gratitude

GROW A PEAR

Daniel Goleman published his book "Emotional Intelligence: Why It Can Matter More Than IQ" in 1995. The book was a best-seller and helped to establish emotional intelligence as a field of study within psychology and management. It covers the concept of emotional intelligence, its relationship with traditional intelligence, and its role in personal and professional success. The book is still widely read today and is considered a classic in the field.

Emotional intelligence theory links to the social component of the biopsychosocial model through the work of various human developmental theorists. Chief among them is Dr. Erik Erikson, who proposed his ideas on the influence of human development on social skills acquisition in his book *Childhood and Society* around 1950. Erikson suggested that humans progress through eight predetermined developmental stages, from infancy to adulthood. At each stage, the individual experiences a psychosocial crisis which may have a positive or negative outcome on personality development. Likewise, the consequence of the result of each step strengthens or weakens the individual's ability to resolve future crises. Erikson proposed that these crises are psychosocial because they involve the psychological needs of the individual (psycho) conflicting with the requirements of society (social). According to the theory, competently completing each stage can produce healthy social behavior and attain essential virtues. Virtues are character strengths that help resolve subsequent crises. Failure to capably resolve a developmental stage can affect the ability to resolve problems in future periods, leading to personality deficits and a practical sense of self.

Sundry philosophies have inspired the theory of emotional intelligence. For example, Zeno of Citium, an ancient contributor to EI, founded Stoicism in Athens in 300 B.C.E. Stoicism favors using restraint, rational thought, self-control, and self-discipline in choice-making. Stoics emphasized goodness and peace of mind learned from living a life of virtue. Emperor Marcus Aurelius is considered Stoicism's most influential adherent and advises we should work towards something greater than ourselves while treating others justly and fairly. The Stoics believed that events unfold either in our control or not. We don't have control over the outcome, only the effort.

Stoicism teaches the value of fortitude to overcome maladaptive thoughts and emotions. The principles of philosophy hold that becoming a clear and unbiased thinker advances the understanding of universal reason (logos). Clear and impartial thinking incorporates physics, the natural world, metaphysics, and ethics. These views demonstrate attitudes toward living life using logic, reasoning, epistemology, and their influence on language. Prudence, justice, fortitude, and temperance form the virtue theory of Stoic ethics.

Michael Cornwall

Stoic philosophy is the muse for modern cognitive therapy. For example, cognitive therapy targets the relationship between the body's alert system and our thoughts about the circumstances, events, and people we encounter. Cognitive therapy seeks to alter the views and perceptions that instigate the body's alarm signals and attempts to mitigate or eliminate excessive, undue stress and anxiety.

Although there is something for everyone in EI theory, these models join to constitute the approach EI takes to enrich daily living through emotional intelligence improvement. EI often appeals to naturally observant, empathic, tolerant, adaptative, and flexible investigators of the mind and body. Curiosity is a hallmark of EI, suggesting a genuine linking between snooping around to solve riddles, particularly those involving our own emotional and behavioral maneuvers, and an uncanny connection with observing them in others. Rational, truth, fact, and science-based thought woven into biopsychosocial awareness comprises EI theory and the human experience as a pairing of the mind and body, not as separate parts and pieces to be understood individually.

Anyone can improve their emotional intelligence. Qualities such as self-awareness, empathy, understanding emotions, assertiveness, regulating emotions, and developing social skills are critical to improvement. Practicing mindfulness can also help, as meditative skills allow for better awareness of thoughts and feelings.

EI improvement can seem like a lot of work.

No one ever drowned in sweat.

1

Grow A Pear

Your emotions are the slaves to your thoughts, and you are the slave to your emotions.—Elizabeth Gilbert, *Eat Pray Love: One Woman's Search for Everything Across Italy, India, and Indonesia*

Imagine a colossal, fully established apple tree. This tree thrives inside your head—a mass of dead and living branches, brown, shriveled leaves coexisting in the warmth of newly formed foliage—a work in progress, weakening and flourishing simultaneously. Imagine dangling from each branch whimsical apples, some covered in the dust of time, committed to their place on the limb, some about to fall away, outliving their usefulness, others only starting to ripen.

This bundle of organic material, the fruits of our life's labors, our repeated experiences supporting the efforts of our active and passive living, its branches storing a myriad of real and imaginary

Fears, our delights, worries, celebrations, uncertainties, and nightmares all to be recalled as needed, at lightning speed.

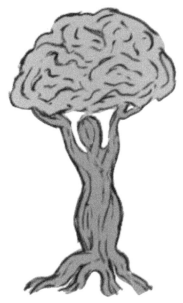

Now imagine a single, shiny pear, green and hopeful, suspended from the arm of one of the craggiest branches, a symbol of life glowing with confidence, shining brightly against the darkness surrounding it.

A pear is growing on the limb of an apple tree!

The complex ecosystem within our skulls, the buffer between us and our encounters with others, is often taken for granted as we search for answers to our emotional problems. Understanding emotion, however, depends on recognizing the immense power of this living, growing, and evolving organ.

The adult brain contains about 100 billion cells linked by branchlike tendrils called dendrites. Within the brain region, where 10,000 brain cells die, and 1,400 new neurons are born every day, branches extend to one another but never touch, forming a tiny space, the synapse, sending chemical messages, dictating which way to go next. It is something like a well-worn path, following the route shown to it by its host after years of instruction. Extensive networks of neurons communicate to generate our thoughts, behaviors, and *memories*. Like well-established limbs that strengthen over time through repeated behavior, like a symphony, makes the structure seemingly impossible to rearrange, dismantle, or obliterate without changing its composition.

Thought, as water to a tree's roots, nourishes its radixes, hardening its bark and forming its branches. As we pour our ideas into the ground around its base, the tree begins as a sapling that can easily shape, reshape, and remake its limbs. As we age, however, the branches formed in our youth become firmer, thicker, and harder to contour. When the tree-like configuration is confidently established (around twenty-five years), we often accept our thoughts as facts—resolute thinking. When practiced over time, our maladaptive habits, self-sabotaging routines, and damaging self-talk stiffen our limbs, leaving them brittle, influencing but not eliminating the potential for improving emotional intelligence.

Many of us rest on the fruits of our labors, even when those fruits have long ago stopped ripening. We are *recidivists*, duplicating the same ways of thinking as if they will someday harvest something more practical. We strengthen this living organ with repeated beliefs, rarely altering our thinking or expressive traditions, stiffening the branches. Although we can always change how we think, the bucket gets lighter the more we feed our brains healthier, more life-sustaining nutrition.

We tend to create a subjective world inside our minds where we rely on a worn-out problem-solving system that turns short-term setbacks into extended losses and temporary pain into long-term suffering. Seemingly afraid of the future, while running from the past, never present, we repeat what is familiar and what feels safe, relying on solutions not to address what is happening but what we believe could, might, and may happen next. Left without alternatives for managing an imagined catastrophe, we continue our routine, reinforcing existing branches without conscious awareness of the damage we are causing ourselves.

Researchers have proposed that humans are born Fearless and acquire their Fears through single or repeated experiences. We can assume humans are content at birth and work tirelessly to destroy that default. Science suggests that Nature does not dictate much to the newborn brain in her deference to evolution and the unexpected.

There may be little prewiring for what we Fear. Only the potential to learn what to Fear and what Not to Fear. Some researchers believe we are born with a Fear of falling, so we avoid that risk in real and symbolic ways. Some philosophers think we're born with two inherent Fears—living alone and being lonely and our distress at being viewed contemptuously by members of our tribes. Science suggests these whispers residing in our cells are present and are derivative of thousands of years of pruning our DNA to predict traits for successful group living.

Our species may have proficiency at birth for cooperation, collaboration, and observing functional rules for copulation among tribe members. (A way of ensuring the traits of cooperation and collaboration are passed on to future offspring.) This genetic sculpting lingers in our modern human design. It is often the basis for extreme

4

fighting, fleeing, or freezing (F^3) when we believe we are weak, unworthy, or no longer have anything to offer our tribe.

"She doesn't like me anymore."

"How is that a problem for you?"

"I'm not sure."

"What do you say to yourself when you think she doesn't like you?"

"Well, I guess I think I'm unlikeable."

"What makes that a problem for you?"

"If I'm unlikeable, no one will like me."

"How do you draw that drastic conclusion?"

"I'm not sure. It's just what I think."

Emotional memory is a shorthand for recalling our experiences and determining whether our recall of the event represented something to Fear or Not to Fear. Our brain cannot remember every detail of our past adventures. It does, however, recall elements of our experiences, but only from our own perspective. So it sorts emotional information into what to recall for survival purposes— what is Fearful and what isn't.

By our design, we hold two expressive potentials.

We are afraid, or we are not afraid.

We can observe children as an example of this phenomenon. Children are not inherently Fearful of bears, lions, or skunks. Take a child to the zoo and watch them grow infatuated with the furry animals behind the high fences. Children will reach for the bear, stare at the orangutan, and imagine cuddling with the cheetah. They will wish for a stuffed replica of a ferocious animal to take home. This curiosity is almost always apparent in how children engage with dinosaurs. We can agree that many dinosaurs were quite dangerous. Children, however, want to ride them and play with them. As children get older, they learn that their initial response to seeing a bear in the zoo may not have been adaptive. So, once we wanted to make friends with bears (FearNot), we began to strengthen that limb and leaf of awareness with another idea: bears can and likely will kill (Fear).

Humans learn what to Fear and what Not to Fear over the first twelve years of development. Our very supple branches take shape during these formative years, and our roots find their way beneath the surface. We learn to differentiate good from bad, best from better, right from wrong, and friend from foe. Snakes, criticism, spiders, ridicule, bats, and rejection each find their place among the branches of our ever-expanding minds and resources for understanding our world. Every branch, limb, and leaf explores the meaning and expression of love, trust, autonomy, industry, and identity, culminating in experience and learning that represents your sense of self.

Memory or recall substantially influences the expression of Fear and FearNot. For example, an actor may draw on real experiences from the past to authentically engage in a role. Likewise, we are actors playing roles, drawing on past experiences to make predictions of ourselves and those around us, perfecting the script, reinforcing the character, and forming our branches.

Emotional intelligence improvement suggests we consider our role or character and the script we read daily and make revisions where necessary. We might explore our memories and what we've learned to Fear and Not to Fear. As time passes, reshaping what we Fear becomes trickier.

The easiest way to identify what you Fear is to bring information into recall by activating events from the past and noticing how your body responds to the thoughts. Your body will let you know if you're afraid by causing uneasiness. A smile, a grimace, or a full-body shake is a dead giveaway.

Short-term memory can recall a small amount of information from a recent period. Can you remember what you ate this morning before starting your day? Long-term memory is the capacity to recall memories from a long time ago. For example, Boston is the capital of England, zebras are insects, and the date of your death are examples of declarative memory. (You just used long-term memory to identify bad examples.) This form of memory contrasts with implicit memory, an indirect, unconscious state.

We often rely on our imagination to construct what we cannot consciously reconstruct. This type of memory is unconscious and unintentional since we cannot deliberately reveal what is not there in our minds without creativity and innovation. Our memories are elaborations, molecular particles of information we add to our stories each time we tell them. Recalling something from long ago is like a fairytale described as a documentary. Recollection is also only a story from the person's perspective. Recall from only one viewpoint cannot give certainty to how we define ourselves through what we've experienced.

How and what we recall using memory is essential to constructing our Fears and *FearNots*. Strengthening branches through repeated experience involves the body's activation of the systems that produce emotional chemicals, the nutrients that build the tree's limbs, and the fruit we grow from the effort.

Suppose a person learns through repeated experience to associate failing with Fear. Neurons will then form around that perception, shaping a cluster, a nucleus, to store information about criticism and its emotional management. We might imagine this as the

7

fruit we produce. Additionally, suppose we repeatedly remind ourselves that a cat is a demon and an elevator is a deathtrap. Because of its immense capacity for imagination, the brain similarly responds to real and imagined threats. We may Fear cats and elevators (and cats on elevators) whenever we encounter these things or imagine them.

As we replay memories through our brains, the connections between neurons associated with recall eventually become a fixed combination. Various regions of the brain help harden the pattern of bonds that form memory and ripen the fruit. Still, memory depends on the solidity of connections between individual brain cells. So if you hear what you perceive as ridicule, for example, you are likely to be flooded with memories you associate with being ridiculed and how you've learned to Fear it or FearNot.

No one place in the brain serves as our memory bank. Instead, we scatter memories over the brain. Many brain cells in several different regions work together to make one memory. For instance, a memory of eating grandma's apple pie might involve some brain cells to help you remember what the pie looked like, others to remember the smell of the cinnamon, and even cells to recognize the delicious taste. In reality, though, memory isn't a physical thing we can find in any given brain cell. It's an action, not an object. Think of baseball fans doing the wave: no single fan is the wave. The magic only happens when all the fans are together, doing their thing in a specific order. In the same way, a memory only happens when many connected neurons fire in a particular pattern. And because the same cells can fire in many unique patterns, one group of neurons can encode multiple memories.

We've suggested that we can view how the neurons communicate as the apple on the tree limb—the fruit of the brain's memory retrieval that ultimately dictates our conclusive perception and the final action. These apples represent what we've learned and relearned when encountering the things we Fear (even their nuances). We rely on repeated patterns of thought and perception to respond to them.

"Don't criticize me! I won't have it!"

"I'm not criticizing you."

"It sounds like criticism."

"It was just an opinion."

"I'm susceptible to criticism. I don't know why."

"I do."

Emotional intelligence concludes that we store the stories, legends, and recollections of situations, circumstances, and people in our cells. This memory relies on the story we told ourselves the last time we recalled it, including each imperfection, exaggeration of detail, and focus on our perspective (and only our perspective). Memory used in this way can be self-destructive and serve no purpose but to prolong and even exaggerate experiences that have ceased to exist except in the imaginative mind.

Magical thinking proposes that one's ideas, thoughts, actions, words, or symbols can influence events in the material world. Magical thinking presumes a causal link between one's inner experience and the external physical environment.

We can use magical thinking to describe ourselves as preyed upon, victims, or survivors. Likewise, we can imagine ourselves as invincible, perfect, and impeccable. Both examples may result in emotional hardship when certainty in oneself becomes debatable. We depend on past experiences to define our fate and who we are. Magical thinking can produce a person who views themselves as helpless, duped, forever feeling regret, damaged, or a fatality, embedding these self-defeating ideas into the brain's cells, creating a mindset that relies on the past to exist at all, playing that role and speaking that script.

Neuroplasticity, or brain plasticity, can be defined as the ability of the nervous system to change its activity in response to intrinsic or extrinsic stimuli by reorganizing its structure, functions, or connections. Brain plasticity depends on the willingness of its host to transform and remodel. Otherwise, this fundamental logic of Nature for growth and development will not often adaptively engage. As brain plasticity is involved, so is the *pruning* away of maladaptive thinking patterns.

Pruning represents the brain's capacity to change, be plastic, reshape, and reinvent itself as situations and circumstances demand. Pruning influences our brain and how it develops, so the thoughts we use, the ideas we practice and repeatedly put into action, become the ones that flourish while others die away. When we change how we think and act, we change the structure of our brain and how we reinvent those neural pathways. If we don't consciously choose which thoughts we're going to keep and which ideas we're going to ignore, then our minds will run wild, like a tree with no care-tender, no plan for growth, or design for sustained living. A single instance redirecting one neuronal impulse in some unmapped direction will influence newer thoughts.

The human brain is the most complex object in the universe, consisting of billions of nerve cells and tiny tree-like structures holding together a massive communication network with enormous computational power. The brain's limb-like neurons pass the thoughts we create to other branches as if playing an elaborate, lightning-quick game of tag, using axons as chasers and dendrites as runners. Neuronal protrusions and spines typically receive the input we create using thought along the stem. These spines contain neurotransmitter receptors, organelles, and signaling systems essential for synaptic function and plasticity, sustaining a structure that relies on thought.

The neurons and dendrites we use the most get thicker and more substantial, like branches on a tree, while the ones we use the least get pruned away, much like trimming the weaker limbs from a developing sapling. Recognizing our potential to reshape, reinvent, and even demolish maladaptive ways of thinking can acknowledge that our imagination of what we have experienced can define us for a lifetime and give substance to our Fears.

The more we flip the script, change our character, and create a new role for ourselves, the more pruning takes place, snipping away the intrusive growth, and avoiding feeding an idea that isn't likely to yield the fruit we'd hoped to produce.

Improved emotional intelligence is like fruit tree grafting, a horticultural technique used to join two living parts of different fruit trees, usually to add desirable characteristics to the host. Grafting is a technique used to combine a desirable rootstock with a scion, a stem, twig, or bud of another tree with desirable fruit-bearing qualities. Grafting can create multi-stemmed trees, produce fruit of one variety on a tree of a different type, and create trees tolerant of unavoidable environmental conditions.

Grafting a pear scion to an apple tree is difficult because apples and pears are from different families of plants, so careful attention to detail is necessary to ensure a bond.

Our shared vision is grafting a new idea onto an older, less fruitful one, creating something new and more adaptive. In the same way, we can imagine changing our thoughts to produce something entirely new.

Something we never dreamed we could do.

In our heads, where we hold the potential for escalating a nightmare into a work of art, fact into fiction, imagination into living, breathing into fire, we can certainly support the fanciful idea that—where there was once an apple on the limb—with effort, we can grow a pear.

No one ever drowned in sweat.

2

No One Ever Drowned In Sweat

Walang gaanong kailangan para magkaroon ng masayang buhay; nasa loob mo ang lahat ng ito, sa iyong paraan ng pag-iisi.

—Marcus Aurelius

There are commonalities in nearly everyone who seeks mental health counseling from my practice. Rarely does anyone know what to expect, but someone told them they needed therapy and mustered the courage (or the insurance coverage) to get it.

Those who see me often claim that *availability* was their first option. After introducing myself, my training, and my licensure, I move into my therapeutic orientation, e.g., the type of therapy I practice. I introduce some basic concepts of EI, asking, "So what are you afraid of today?"

It's a way of jumping right in.

The stare is familiar.

"Afraid? I'm not afraid of anything."

"From my experience, people who seek therapy are afraid of something and want help identifying their Fears. We will learn some skills around that idea."

"I was hoping to understand my childhood better, and I have some unfinished business I need to understand."

"What is in your past that can bring you peace?"

"I've been mistreated."

"Can you change that?"

"No."

"What is there to understand about it?"

"I just thought that's the way these things work."

"We don't do that here. All the answers you seek are in this moment, in the thoughts you hold about the past—not the past itself."

The human brain is a thriving, tree-like structure with fruit, leaves, and scattered growth. I consider it my duty to help my clients prune away the past debris and promote new growth as soon as possible, mainly before their insurance runs out, and all we have to show for our efforts is a long, repetitive journey into the past.

"I cannot live with the memories."

"Are you being mistreated now?"

When my patients arrive, I imagine them carrying bushels of tortured, bruised, battle-worn apples—the fruit of their thoughts. Rarely do they have any idea what to do with it all, lugging it around for a lifetime, forever weighed down by the surplus of past harvests.

"Here, let me help you with those. Looks heavy," I imagine myself saying.

"There are a few more full baskets in the car."

"Why don't we begin with these? It seems like you have enough already."

"But we are missing the best ones. You have to see them all to understand me fully," continues the imagined plea, tubs of apples overflowing and landing on the floor. "I haven't had *closure,* and I need to understand."

"I think we have enough to get a good picture."

"I don't know where to begin if I don't tell the whole story from the beginning."

"Did you happen to read my website?" I politely ask, "Do you know what kind of therapy I practice?"

"MmmmmmmmmNnnnnnnno," they often say, apples scattered everywhere by now, "I didn't know there were types of therapy," suddenly drowning in apples, "What do you mean?"

"Did you look at the website at all?"

"No, I just wanted a quick appointment."

People regularly expect to engage in therapy with me, similar to what they see in movies or TV. They may believe mental health clinicians provide a mystical, magical adventure into the past, discovering the hidden meaning, a clearer picture of the terrible events of their childhood, and what it was all about back then.

I imagine myself and my overburdened companion preparing to dig through piles and piles of bruised and dusty apples, scanning each one to explain *why* we behave as we do. Never *how* we make ourselves feel in the moment. "I found a clue! Why didn't I see it there?" I imagine them shouting.

I ask, "What shall we do with it?"

"It's the answer to why I'm so depressed!"

"Well, in that case, your depression is now cured!"

"I'm still depressed."

"Shall we dig deeper?"

"Yes! I know the clue to my depression is here somewhere."

"Emotional intelligence," I say, awakening from my dream and returning my mind to the moment, "I practice emotional intelligence theory. Do you know this idea? Emotional intelligence improvement?"

"No," is the customary reply, "sounds complicated. *Intelligence*? I'm not the sharpest knife in the block, bulb in the socket, apple in the crate."

"It's not that kind of intelligence."

Oddly, when I declare my practice orientation, people quickly give me a gauge of their imagined intelligence. They often say, "I'm not very good at that," as if married to a poem or script and couldn't be better at anything they are not already an expert.

It may be that when we hear the word *intelligence*, we tense, relying on our presumed definition of the phrase *intelligence quotient* (IQ) for clarity. Some illusionary gauge of intellect. One of the many methods for defining people and their learning potential. A gauge we often use to determine self-acceptance and integrity.

"I will explain," I say, "Simple idea. Just a little more difficult to set in motion."

"Goodness, is there a test? I don't do very well on tests."

"How do you know that?" I ask.

"Experience," I hear, "I always fail tests."

"Can you describe yourself more fairly?"

"Not really."

Although the concepts of IQ and EI are similar, there are some main differences. Unlike IQ, something believed to be fixed at birth, embedded in DNA, and a measure of intellectual potential, EI is a self-defined assessment of emotional adaptability, both as a distinct individual and a member of society. EI is far more flexible than IQ and can improve with effort. We may quickly gauge our EI by how we answer a few simple questions:

Am I content with how I address criticism?

Am I confident and hopeful when I fail?

Do I respond adaptively to inconvenience?

Am I future-focused, afraid of what will happen next?

Am I past-focused, reminding myself of my regrets?

Do I have a Fear of bursting into flames?

Do I criticize others more than I examine myself?

In contrast to IQ, EI relies on brain plasticity, or the ability of the brain to modify itself and its wiring organically. Without the adaptability found in brain plasticity, any brain, not just the human brain, would be unable to develop from infancy to adulthood, learn, or recover from brain injury.

EI relies on the flexibility of the brain to adapt.

Fairly assessing our skills in emotional management is the primary model for identifying opportunities for improvement in EI. We can include reports from others and their ideas about our abilities to identify opportunities for EI improvement. However, as previously stated, improvement is an objective self-measurement that encourages continued review.

The design of EI self-assessment isn't to reimagine the past or imagine the future to engage with now. On the contrary, we can expect an EI self-assessment to be unbiased, open-minded, and ongoing, focusing on monitoring progress, identifying weaknesses and strengths as we go, opportunities for self-acceptance, and potential for real-time solutions.

When I answer, I consider the individual before me, "Emotional intelligence improvement relies on fact, truth, and science to draw conclusions about ourselves, others, and circumstances. You can learn how to do that if you decide to return." I sit and wait for an expression of interest. "We don't often examine the past by reliving it. We may revisit it for a moment or two to get useful information, but it isn't where EI improvement occurs. EI emphasizes the *here-and-now*, is solution-focused, and is not heavy on storytelling. Our goal is awareness of this moment, our self-talk, and what we can do about our problems at the moment." I observe the apples fading slightly, making room, watching for the individual to sit back and relax, loosening the grip on the bushel basket.

"I've never heard of that," they may say, "I'm interested."

I observe what may have once been a hopeless situation as an opportunity full of potential. The patient becomes a student. "It's a bottom-up therapy type," I say, "We don't begin fixing our heads or thoughts. We begin by managing the body first." I point at my toes, move toward my head, and point at my temple. "You can't fix a nutty head with a nutty head because you'll get more nutty thoughts. It's like a dog chasing its tail. When we cannot manage the thoughts that generate emotion, we manage the body first to calm the toes up, making rational thinking more possible by eliminating or weakening the impact of the stress hormones in our bloodstream."

"How do I do that?" I hear.

"You've done something already," I say. "You changed your need to know *why* to learn *how*. How do I make myself feel? Never why am I feeling this way? Leave the whys to fiction writers. Seek to know how you make yourself feel the way you do. There is so much more benefit in that goal."

Our brains hold immense potential for extinguishing self-sabotaging emotional behavior. Our drive to adapt influences the brain's structure and function and can help produce more adaptive, less self-destructive emotional outcomes. We can destroy our emotional lives by relying on folk psychology and its inherent lack of insight and initiative for improvement or drop anchor in sanity and reason through EI improvement.

EI theory operationalizes the emotional potential each of us possesses to live without unnecessary stress. Practice, determination, and confident desire can produce anger, hatred, and depression, while the same effort can promote expressions of contentedness and acceptance. Of course, some stress motivates us, but we produce the most pressure using imagination and catastrophic, future-focused thought.

"This sounds like a lot of work. I might be too far gone for this. I'm a lot like my mother and have a temper."

"It isn't easy, but no one ever drowned in sweat," I say.

EI emphasizes the benefits of self-acceptance, particularly the observance of one's character points that, like IQ, are more related to genetics than skill-building and relearning. We are connected to our genetic temperament and personality, accepting our unique design before attempting to modify it.

Personality traits are complex and shaped by both inheritance and environment. Nature and nurture play an essential role in the expression of personality. When genetics influences our behavior, no matter how hard we try to reshape it through practice, we may be left exhausted and confused instead of changed and renewed. To change an individual's personality is much like asking them to change their eye color. It isn't possible, so we are left to accept where change is not likely. We can, however, always change our behavior in relation to our personality. For instance, if our character is shy and introverted, we may choose to stay in the house and fear social events. The personality is steadfast and is not changeable. The behavior—the fear of going outdoors and socializing—can indeed be modified through managed thinking, thought challenging, and practice.

EI suggests we are open to changing the goal but always willing to change the plan. When our genetic personality overrides our will to improve in a particular direction, self-acceptance and patience may be the best strategy for EI improvement.

If genetics influences how we respond to the events of our lives, we can learn to have patience with our initial response to hardship and harsh conditions. When we behave contrary to our plan, recognizing that we can form a second thought about our first thought, we utilize our potential for improvement and our patience for self-acceptance and self-tolerance.

As we seek to improve our EI, we will continue to make mistakes, and sometimes we will make the same mistake repeatedly. We may have to learn to be less self-damning, fault-finding and disturbed in our efforts to gauge our achievements in EI improvement.

We can accept our natural character traits and summon an authentic and sincere self-apology instead of self-destruction, growling when inconvenienced, impeded, or blocked. We might also acknowledge our tendency to make less-than-flattering choices when facing a dispute and hope to behave better when similar situations arise. Not to make our character dictate certainty but to hope for something less self-damaging and more self-assuring.

Like IQ, emotional intelligence is thinking and perceiving using adaptive insight and corresponding behavior. EI is a particular kind of *self-and-other awareness* that can take a lifetime to develop. EI can improve our physical and emotional lives, but only when confidence, patience, and the willingness to fail overrules the potential for gain. EI emphasizes that it is not the outcome we pursue but the process.

I return my focus to my client. "I raised three children, and one isn't doing so well," she says.

"What do you imagine that means about you?" I say, careful not to step too heavily on her wreckage.

"Well, it has to mean something for something, doesn't it?"

"What makes this idea important to you?"

"My children are all grown," she said, "Two of them are doing pretty damn good." She reaches for two of the best apples and holds them for me to admire. She breathes onto them and shines them on her shirt sleeve.

"What does their success mean about you?"

"I think it means I'm a *good* mother. Except for the youngest, I didn't do well with that one." She motions to a craggy apple sitting atop her head.

Estimations of EI, much like IQ, rely on comparison to others. For example, a person who performs poorly on a standardized IQ test can face criticism from peers, employers, and social encounters. Estimating our learning potential can lead to an individual resenting learning, avoiding risk, and believing that they are more likely to fail.

Likewise, a *good* mother is often the result of meeting certain social expectations. From this perspective, self-acceptance can become quite unachievable without a perfect contrast.

"What do your child's mistakes mean about you?" I ask.

Her eyes look toward the most miserable apple balanced precariously above. "I'm a bad mother."

"You just said you're a good mother. Which is it?"

"I guess I'm bad because I didn't succeed entirely."

"Prove it," I say. "Prove to me that your children define your human worth."

Many parents, particularly mothers, identify as *good* if their children do well and are reasonable compared to other children. If not, parents may believe they are *bad*, leaving only their children's choices throughout life to estimate their worth as parents. Instead of shining brighter than their least brilliant child, many parents will occupy the space beside them to help them manage to fail. *We are both failures, honey. Don't feel so bad. I'm suffering with you.*

EI rejects the idea that people can be good or bad. People will be works in progress until they die. Being bad would be like determining whether a shirt is unwearable because it is missing a button. EI endorses self-acceptance, often the result of an internal, rational debate, a fact-based decision-making process when concluding decisions about oneself and others. We can conclude that a shirt without a button is undoubtedly wearable and possesses a charm unlike any other if we view the shirt from this perspective.

Like IQ, EI can be persuaded by how we rely on comparison to define our self-worth. Although comparison does play a role in social adaptability, often influencing our definitions of good, bad, better, best, friend, foe, right, and wrong, the extent to which we compare ourselves to others can strengthen or weaken our foundation of EI. Mainly when our human value depends on how well or unwell we compare to others, our ideas about ourselves, our confident beliefs, morals, and values, and our internal capacity for self-acceptance eventually erode.

Often referred to as an *external locus of control,* destabilized emotional intelligence may lie in our determination to compare ourselves. Self-worth (or self-acceptance) derives from how much trust we place in our judgment, often expressed in the willingness to engage in things we may fail. In fact, confidence has a direct relationship with one's willingness to fail. If you are afraid to fail, for fear of being a failure, you will never try anything new or unusual.

Self-acceptance can lead to greater autonomy in decision-making. We can, in this way, establish a foundation for more manageable self-acceptance when we take risks (with the possibility of failing) and encounter potential criticism without Fear. Likewise, in establishing self-acceptance, we can build a foundation for accepting others as imperfect and redeemable as we do ourselves.

"Was this the plan you had for your life? To be a perfect mother and a wife?" I ask.

"I guess it was what people expected."

"What were your expectations?"

"It all happened too fast for that."

"What did you expect from that decision?"

"To be a perfect wife and mother."

"Did that happen?"

"No."

"What does that mean about you in this moment?"

If you believe you are unintelligent, averse to risk-taking, less capable of self-restraint, and more likely to fail, you will be forever anxious, Fearing harsh judgment, and viewed as a failure.

A nincompoop!

Incapable!

If you believe you could improve your EI, it's likely true. We can establish self-satisfying goals if we learn to accept ourselves as we are, without achievement, relying on our judgment and not how we will compare and contrast with others if we choose our route.

This type of self-assessment involves making thought-provoking yet honest observations of ourselves without comparison. These questions and the gathered information can support improvement in emotional intelligence, primarily when used intentionally to shape behavior, character, and reputation.

EI is a continuous self-assessment and improvement strategy that relies on insight and individual preference. Everyone experiences setbacks in EI improvement, but those who take the time to learn from mistakes and begin again succeed the most.

It's not easy to develop the kind of self-awareness most helpful in improving EI. Kindness, acceptance, and patience, both with ourselves and others, play a significant role in making self-awareness and self-acceptance a lifelong goal.

It may mean we can make choices and set goals without damning ourselves for not behaving to our plan every time. When we act counter to our strategies, self-acceptance can help reduce or prevent careless decision-making, impulsive behavior, and imprudent choices, which often compound the issue we attempt to manage.

Our moral self-regard may influence the choices made by others about us. When we are in a self-and-other acceptance mindset, we are more likely to convince and persuade ourselves to find the truth, fact, and science in our choices.

EI emphasizes the *how* involved in emotional expression rather than the *why*. EI does not emphasize exploring the past or understanding the *why* of emotional expression. It is more often the question: *How do I make myself feel that way?* Rather than attempting an answer to *Why do I feel this way?* EI improvement focuses on thought happening here and now, not reimagining the past and examining it for hidden meaning. We may use some storytelling in the present-focused EI practice as a reference point, with little emphasis lingering there. Here-and-now therapies don't believe anything hidden would help manage the present moment. Reimagining the past can often be a source of anxiety and depression.

I focus my attention back on my client. "I had a bad childhood, and I wanted to be better at mothering than my mother," she said, wiping a tear away, "I guess I didn't do so well."

"What are you thinking about when you remember your childhood? When you compare yourself to your mother?" I ask.

"I think it shouldn't have happened that way," she said, gathering apples and holding them to her chest, "Abuse and neglect are not how parents should treat children."

"How should children be treated?"

"They should grow up healthy and loved."

"Was that the case for you?"

"No!"

"What does that *mean* about you *now,* at this moment, that you didn't have a trouble-free childhood?" There is a pause. "If your parents mistreated you, what does that *mean* about you *now*? Right now?"

"It means I missed out. It means my parents broke me. It means I'm not good enough. It means my parents shouldn't have been abusive. It means I am a victim!"

"What does it mean about you *now*, at this moment, that you've been a victim?"

"I'm still a victim."

There is not often a quick dénouement to a session involving this topic. It takes a while to coax people into the moment and untie the words and phrases used for years to manage their thoughts. It isn't easy to enter the story from a different angle where facing problems is the focus, rather than racing around a track that, over time, becomes a well-trodden and reflexive trail to victimhood and even survivor hood.

The mother sitting in front of me, whose past experiences and youngest son somehow defines her worth, is awaiting my response. "It could be that your childhood and your son's choices can mean something *to* you," I say, "without meaning something *about* you if you want to improve your emotional intelligence."

"I never thought of it that way." She reaches for the mangy apple sitting on her head and examines it. "What my son does means something *to* me, but it doesn't mean anything *about* me." She sits and thinks for a moment. "I like that, and it makes better sense." She takes a bite of her apple and smiles. "This tastes like a pear," she says.

"If you changed the narrative to what it means *to* you instead of what it means *about* you, what conclusions could you draw instead?"

"I'm sorry I was treated that way, but I'm not being treated that way anymore. Unless I reimagine it and tell myself it shouldn't have been that way. And my son makes the decisions he makes, and they are not about me. I taught him good, bad, better, best, right, wrong, friend and foe. That's all I could do." Some of her apples disappear into thin air, and others remain. "I have to change the way I think about things." She pauses. "This is going to be a lot of work."

No one ever drowned in sweat.

3

Le Plat Principal

Don't be more cowardly than children, but just as they say,
when the game is no longer fun for them, 'I won't play anymore,' you
too, when things seem that way to you, say, 'I won't play anymore,' and
leave, but if you remain, don't complain. — (Discourses I.24.20)

Emotional intelligence (EI) theory is one practice model for addressing whole-person wellness. EI theory is a *lifestyle*, not an issue-specific modality for resolving immediate emotional discomfort. It is a mindset with a plan to encounter emotional struggles using its prescribed skills, techniques, and philosophies willingly and confidently, regardless of the event itself. EI welcomes unpleasantness alongside agreeableness as they are perceptions that both can instigate curiosity.

EI offers a plan for daily living. Unlike other counseling theories, EI does not routinely focus on specific problems, e.g., job loss, the death of a loved one, or objectionable encounters with others. Instead those interested in EI as a way of life (those we shall call *practitioners*) examine how they made themselves content, accepting, and relaxed as dexterities in managing setbacks and emotional discomfort.

Practitioners of EI view emotional problem-solving as less specific to an event and more of an opportunity to discover the foundations of thinking and how thinking influences more than just the problem at hand. Thoughts interconnect and affect one another, resulting in an impact on the whole person. For example, if we think we aren't worth it, we may feel depressed, stay on the couch all day, overeat and lose hope. Likewise, the same thought can impact our career goals, friendships, intimate relationships, and overall health.

In contrast, if we believe hopefully, reasonably, and self-approvingly, we might reject the idea that we are worthless (because the assumption cannot be supported using evidence) and accept the risks inherent in building relationships or seeking more rewarding employment. Our self-worth, we may discover, isn't found in how we perform but in what we think about our performance.

EI theory views emotion as resembling a spider's web. The web's threads spread in all directions and influence the whole structure. Locating the hub or center of a trap is the goal of the EI practitioner. For instance, we may complain of depression after splitting with a mate. The goal is often to discover the Fear that compels believing that losing a partner is a catastrophe. The EI practitioner will view this problem as something more profound, digging deeper than the event to

29

touch on wider-ranging assumptions about the meaning of parting with a loved one.

We may believe that the end of a relationship means we will be alone and lonely forever and that the remainder of our life is a catastrophe. We may think we're not good enough or unworthy of having a relationship with anyone when we lose a friend. Our imagined destiny is loneliness, that love is not in the cards for us, and we should give up on love altogether before destroying ourselves again.

Instead of consoling ourselves by suggesting that a new relationship is just around the corner to replace the lost love, enabling the idea to perpetuate, the EI practitioner would dig a few shovelfuls deeper and ask more self-probing questions: *What does it mean about me at this moment to be alone? What makes being alone a problem for me? What do I tell myself about being alone? How does being alone now predict the rest of my life? What are the statistical odds and the likelihood that I will remain single forever? But even if I defy the odds and stay alone forever, what would that mean about me?*

These questions may uncover something more weighty than just breaking up with a partner. For instance, we may respond to these questions: *Is it true that I am no good unless I have someone who loves me in my life? Can I prove that I have to call someone my own to be content in my life? To be a worthwhile human being, is it a fact that I must have someone waiting for me at home when I open the front door? If I am alone, is that proof enough that I am unworthy? Do I need to be loved by someone else to feel good about myself?* These conclusions are more likely the root of the problem and would be the aim for EI improvement through disputation of the assumptions we feed our minds. Later chapters will discover how to dispute these self-defeating thoughts using Stoic reasoning and Ellis's ABC model for practical, emotional management.

While EI theory improves individual emotional problem-solving by building body-mind awareness, it focuses on *mindfulness* to manage both body and mind systems, joining them to improve overall health.

EI theory promotes mindfulness and teaches practitioners to address the events of their lives in the present moment, not using imagination, magic, or decorative thought to organize thinking. EI practitioners strive to encounter emotional difficulties, not as we imagine them in the future but as they unfold at the moment. The promotion of inner peace is when we recognize that we have nothing to apologize for and nothing to Fear.

Mindfulness is intensely sensing and feeling without interpretation or judgment. EI improvement focuses on the very moment of life and our immediate thoughts in it. By connecting the primary challenge to present thinking, the practitioner may eliminate imagined obstacles, improve insight, engage in solution-focused problem-solving, and establish a better range of skills to resolve inevitable emotional challenges later.

Practicing mindfulness inspires breathing awareness, guided imagery, and other techniques for relaxing the body and mind. The challenge isn't swimming into the darkness of the past or the murky uncertainty of the future. It is to return to shore, where real-time, solution-focused skill-building awaits. For example, an individual may complain of anxiety related to an impending job loss or perceived future peril, risk, or danger. The individual may point to a supervisor as the source of the anxiety.

"If I only had a different boss."

"It seems you imagine losing your job or being better off if things were not as they are."

"Well, everything points to it."

"Everything except that you have a job right now, and you are scaring yourself to death with your imagination of what will happen if you lose it. You dream of how things would be better if they were not the way they are, and you imagine dragons await you where there are none. You live in the future."

"Sounds right."

"If you did not use the past or the future to describe your problems—if you focused only on this moment and not on reimagining your past or forecasting doom in your future, what problems would you truly have?"

"If I didn't think about the past or the future when I think of this problem, I wouldn't have any problems."

"Exactly."

"What about planning for things? How do I do that?"

"Flexible planning includes the idea that the future is unknown and that plans can and likely will change, depending on the information we have at the moment. Inflexible plans that cannot shape to the facts of the moment will not likely benefit achieving your goals." I look for understanding. "Goals are not often straight lines from start to finish. When we set goals, we have to consider more of a zig-zag pattern. If we believe our path to our goal must be a straight line, we will give up or experience anxiety with each effort."

"Why do I live in the past?"

"You live in the past because it's a minefield of excuses to explain what you are not willing to do now."

The practitioner may use the presenting complaint to identify the foundation of the problem, labeling it *anticipatory anxiety,* future-focused imagination, and catastrophic thinking.

"If I lose my job, I won't pay my bills!"

"How do you know that?"

"It makes sense to me, and I will have to move and be homeless, and it would be terrible."

"When we imagine the future, we can't rely on that artistic detail to predict it. When you imagine dragons, you could use a more reliable measurement. Think of the shape of a bell curve instead. There are extreme ends, and you have many possibilities in the middle. You seem to be going to only one end of the spectrum and using only minimal information. You are drawing conclusions using only the idea that the outcome will be catastrophic. What are the chances, opportunities, probabilities, and statistical likelihood that you will not find another job and be homeless if you lose your job?"

"When you put it that way, I think I'm in the middle. In some ways, I'm closer to the right tail. The chances are pretty good, and I will find another job *if I need one.* It won't be the most pleasurable thing I have ever had to do. Maybe I will throw some lines in the water and see what I reel in. I probably wouldn't be so needy about my job if I did that."

"It is likely and probable that you could have some discomfort if you transition from something familiar to something new. We don't know. But will you bleed? Will you die? Or will you handle it as you've handled everything so far in your life?"

"It's probable that I will handle it if it happens."

"What else can you do?"

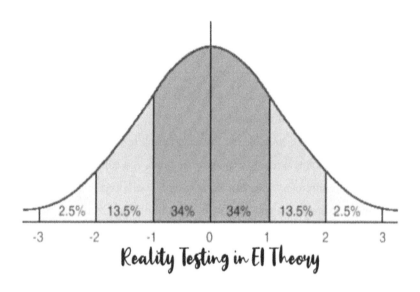

| 2.5% | 13.5% | 34% | 34% | 13.5% | 2.5% |

-3   -2   -1   0   1   2   3

Reality Testing in EI Theory

Improved awareness of the role of thinking and perception on emotional expression may lead to a broader understanding of how thought and perception, principally future-focused, catastrophic thinking, impact the brain, body, and social living. These are the main ideas in EI theory, ideas not often considered collectively in other emotional problem-solving strategies.

Like preparing a soup, EI theory incorporates unique ingredients in its composition, each element identifiable with every spoonful. A mixture of truth, fact, and science, precisely served.

EI theory has a distinct and noticeable flavor. You may prefer something colder, hotter, spicier, or mixed from a bag or a can to add water and serve.

When shopping for a recipe, remember that the best soups are built from testing, creating a winning harmonization of flavors.

Likewise, never forget that continuing dining is the left diner's judgment.

You may have already been alerted to whether you will develop a taste for EI theory or pass on it. As we continue to unfold the theory, your appetite may improve.

One serving of EI theory may not give the diner enough to make a competent judgment.

You may need a second helping for balance.

Or throw it all out and start again.

No one ever drowned in sweat.

4

Our Lives In Trees

Three musts hold us back: I must do well. You must treat me well. And the world must be easy. —Albert Ellis

Humans likely lived in trees for the majority of our species' existence. Anthropologists believe humans lived in trees for over two million years, constructing treehouses, huts, and other structures to live and sleep under the canopy. We came down from trees after assessing the enriched opportunities for collaboration and cooperation with others, not to mention the improved copulative prospects earth-bound living could deliver. Equally, it is generally more dangerous for humans to live in trees. Although handy for short periods of protection from predators who cannot climb as well as we do, tree habitats usually lack the stability and security from natural disasters that living on the ground provides. Additionally, tree living requires a high level of stamina and coordination and can be physically dangerous without careful planning and construction. Not to mention the energy and strength needed to maintain balance.

Although we've descended the trees, we still prefer to keep an eye on our predators from some vantage point above, observing, giving us protection and time to plan our next move.

Our threats have changed, too, replaced almost entirely by our imaginations of the future or the past. We imagine what will happen next and reimagine what has happened already. And we suffer the consequences of the answers only limited by our inventiveness, originality, and the fertility of our imagination. We have lost the protection of trees but surrounded ourselves with imaginative, more powerful, angrier monsters in the process.

Imagination is a powerful tool. It is also the primary source of anxiety and depression. The mind only knows what we tell it. When we invent something happening or not happening or how we will handle a situation in the future, our minds can become overwhelmed by worry, uncertainty, and Fear, all inspired by imaginative thought.

The body's alert system responds to real and invented threats. When we visualize a potential danger (future-focused), the brain can automatically and unconsciously signal our body to activate the fight, flight, or freeze (F^3) response. As a result, the body may produce physiological changes to prepare us to inhibit or energize movement depending on the perceived threat. These changes can include increased heart rate, blood pressure, respiration, blood flow to the limbs, the release of stress hormones like cortisol, and alertness. Many of us live in this chronic state of anxiety, fueled entirely by the fictions of the mind.

People have become more isolated in recent years due to the rise of technology and the fact that many live in larger cities. People spend more time in front of screens or in their homes and less time in their communities. The *gig* economy's growth—a labor market heavily influenced by independent contractors rather than permanent employees, has decreased meaningful work-life relationships. People have focused more on short-term work projects, makeshift relationships, and technology-bound friendships. Increased anxiety about safety in public spaces has also made people more hesitant to leave their homes and interact with others. In many ways, we have returned to living in trees.

We are more Fearful of the future—stress resulting from the expectation of an event or situation and the Fear that one is unprepared for it. We might call this anticipatory anxiety—when we imagine every terrible consequence and outcome and how we expect to handle it. We envision every possible horrible outcome hundreds of times a day. This neverending response to an imagined disaster can become an issue when it is excessive or chronic. Common symptoms of anticipatory anxiety may include difficulty concentrating, feeling overwhelmed, Fear of the unknown, and avoidance of a situation.

Conversely, retrospective depression, is a type of depression that occurs when an individual looks back on their life and realizes how different it is from what they hoped or expected it to be. Failed relationships may cause missed opportunities or a lack of personal accomplishments. The symptoms of retrospective depression include low self-esteem, guilt, regret, and sadness.

Because our modern-day threats are primarily invented, humankind has returned to living in trees, leaving us no way to climb down and resume our regular lives. We remain there, perched on the limbs, hidden among the fruits and nuts, terrified of uncertainty, risk, and the imagined outcomes of climbing down. Our new predators are bills, lines, and old age; we panic when in love and agonize when alone. We dread ridicule, judgment, and criticism. We say we want to float above the clouds, yet we hunker down and only peek through the leaves.

In trees, we have few relationships, believing human attachment and bonding lead only to insecurity and long-term despair. We *need* what we could *want*, Fear the future, feel distressed over losing control and ignore the present moment and its possibilities. We learn that lasting comfort is only a pill, a drink, or a gamble away. We work at home, safe in our nests, and receive our essentials by mail. We are impatient with ourselves, so we are impatient with others. We are suspicious because we lack confidence. We Fear the first step—seeking reassurance that the third step will be better than the second.

Our human design is to pursue daily life in homeostatic balance, an automatic process by which biological systems maintain stability while adjusting to surrounding conditions—the point when we rest, renew and recover (R^3). Still, we can quickly engage in the fight, freeze, or flee response (F^3) to preserve life depending on the state of our minds.

Thousands of years ago, when it was common to run into a hungry predator, the F^3 gave us the zing to scramble into a tree for safety. We'd sit in the limbs and wait for the prowler to wander away, signifying that it was time to risk descent and resume our lives.

The perception of threat also activates the F^3. Imagining that something *might* happen activates the same protective system and prepares us to face imagined danger or run from it. It is this system, in modern times, that keeps us in trees. The consequence of relying on imaginative thought to keep us safe hijacks the entire operation of the body and mind, making rational thinking and managed behavior nearly impossible. Unlike our earliest ancestors who waited for a sign that the threat had gone hunting another prey, today, we are left sitting in trees, never believing that we are safe enough to come down.

"What if that happens?"

"Yes! It could happen."

"Let's just stay up here where it's safe."

"Just in case."

"It looks safe, but I'm sure there's something else hiding in the brush."

"We'd better just stay put."

"You never know!"

"We might starve."

"We can call for delivery."

The human brain alerts us to what we tell it. Thoughts about criticism, undesirability, bankruptcy, and loneliness send messages to the F^3, producing stress hormones and directing us to search for cover.

"My girlfriend broke up with me!"

"How is that a problem for you?"

"I will be alone!"

"What makes that a problem for you?"

"I *need* a girlfriend to be happy."

"Prove it."

After climbing into our imaginary tree and returning to our pre-arousal, homeostatic balance can take a lifetime—mainly because we fuel our Fear with thoughts of what *could* happen if we let our guards down.

In the past, our recovery time correlated with how long it took the predator to wander away. Now, because our dragons are primarily figments of our imagination, the threat never goes away. We quickly replace one terror with another fictional threat—a hungrier wolf, an angrier neighbor, a life-dooming grade, a hopeless marriage, or an endless job search.

Unless we work in a high-risk job, most of us have few true dangers to manage in our daily lives—unless we imagine the future or reimagine the past. In place of real threats, we perform victim rehearsals of what the future could be or what the past has been, the fiction of the mind we teach ourselves. Daily life, from this perspective, makes pauses in the stress response few and far between.

Phobias are good examples of misuse of the F^3 and the false information we use to activate it. A person who thinks terrifying thoughts about high places might fabricate stress while standing at a window in a skyscraper. The body responds to the mind's messages, e.g., *I'm panicking! What if I lose control? What if I have to ask a stranger for help? What if I'm dying? What if I have a heart attack?*

Thought makes the body alert, releasing stress hormones and increasing heartbeat and respiration. Equally, we are prone to rethink our Fearful thoughts, restarting the stress hormone flushing hundreds of times in a row. Panic can result from this exaggerated, invented threat by intensifying Fear, causing a more intense release of stress hormones for Fear of losing control or even dying.

When we examine our thinking, we would likely find that we associate high places and windows with terror, blaming our Fear of high places and windows instead of our imagination's role in the Fear. It is not the windows or high places that instigate our F^3. It is our thoughts about windows and high places. For instance, if it were the windows or the high places that caused the Fear, everyone would feel Fear when in the same situation, leaving the activity of skydiving, mountain climbing, and airplane travel an obstacle to that logic. It is not the situation that causes Fear. It is our thoughts about it.

It is crucial to recognize that Fear does not come at you—it comes from you. Even face-to-face with a skunk, the F^3 would not activate without imagination. We would have to envision what the skunk *would do*, not what the skunk is doing; even if the skunk sprays us, our vision of recovering from the spray fuels our Fear response even more.

Understanding the body's natural response to Fearful thoughts is one way to help shorten our time sitting in trees. The threats that keep us out on a limb will not manifest without creativity and self-destructive inventiveness.

If a rabid dog is chasing you, you should use the F^3 and throw a rock, growl, or climb a tree and wait for it to go away. Otherwise, without actual threat, rational thought can make our lives in trees more choice than the default.

Day after day, we nest in the limbs of trees, with no idea when it's safe to come down, stuck there, relying on our image of the terrors that await us if we do, gripping us to our perch. We dream (if we could only fall asleep) that if we wait long enough, we will have that carefree life we know is somewhere, other than where we are, just waiting for us. In the meantime, we squander our precious, finite lifetime imagining dragons. Slaying one problem, engaging in another, watching as the slain come back to life, grow ten heads, and bring ten drunken friends.

Anticipatory anxiety is a normal reaction, but there are some strategies to help people manage it. People can start by recognizing and validating their feelings and learning to identify their thoughts. It's also helpful to create a plan to address the situation, practice relaxation techniques such as deep breathing, and try to focus on the present moment.

Emotional intelligence plays a significant role in managing anticipatory anxiety. Emotionally intelligent people tend to respond to life in a balanced and thoughtful way. They can recognize and understand their own emotions and the emotions of others and use this information to guide their thoughts and actions. They can regulate their feelings and respond to challenges and difficult situations calmly and effectively. They also tend to have good social skills and can build and maintain genuine relationships. Overall, emotional intelligence is a crucial factor in reducing anticipatory anxiety.

Improvement in EI begins with self-assessment, analyzing and evaluating one's present ability with emotional management, and determining that growth is possible. We might start our quest by asking, *Could I be less impulsive with my thoughts and actions? Can I manage emotional expression more proactively? Can I climb down from my tree, confident that I will most assuredly handle whatever (if anything) lies below?*

If your answer is *No*, then you're okay!

If your answer is *Maybe*, surely you tease.

If your answer is *Yes*, the slog begins.

We will now quibble with the details.

EI could better fit within the framework of an aptitude, a talent—curiosity with legs. These dexterities may lead to an improved capacity to face any crisis with lower levels of stress, less emotional reactivity, and fewer unintended consequences.

EI is an option for anyone willing to embark on any goal, sacrificing emotional routine for more adaptive habits. To do something you've not done before to achieve something unexpected. Improved EI is grounded in accepting risk, without which emotional intelligence may remain unchanged, save the ravages of time.

Emotional intelligence theory offers an alternative to imagining dragons and proposes that *being* fully requires accepting the enormous risk of living. We can use truth, fact, and science to conclude our response to issues we face *at the moment*, exactly as our ancestors did thousands of years ago, and we can make better decisions when we have the facts present only at the moment. Of course, we can make plans, but they must be flexible and adjust with time as new information accumulates.

"What if this happens?"

"Yes! You're right! What if that happens?"

"I never thought of that. What if this happens?"

We can add that we will handle anything we encounter to our prediction. The projection, however, can be exhaustive using imagination. EI suggests making more flexible yet functional predictions using statistical judgment, probability, and data about our predictions:

"What if that happened?"

"There's a molecular chance that would happen. It could happen, but it isn't likely."

"What about this?"

"Seems granular."

"This is no fun. It's more work."

"That's probable."

The great philosopher Winnie the Pooh writes of his walk with Piglet through Hundred Acre Wood: *Supposing a tree fell, Pooh, when we were underneath it? ' Pooh paused, 'Supposing it didn't,' said Pooh after careful thought. Piglet was comforted by this.*

We can always use *Words of Winnie* to derive the essential ideas to improve EI. Open any of A.A. Milne's books to a random page, and you will find immense knowledge in fewer words than I currently use.

We can expect to improve EI through insight and curiosity into whole-person operations. EI practitioners begin that process by acknowledging that the primary cause of emotional disturbance originates in our beliefs about ourselves, others, and the world around us. EI proposes that irrational beliefs are the foundation of prolonged stress arousal and emotional anguish, contributing to physical illness, disease, and death.

We can climb down from the trees and engage in life by accepting the risk inherent in any undertaking. We can handle not knowing the future to the detail we demand by making flexible plans without relying on uncompromising, imaginative outcomes.

We can take anything if we encounter challenges as they come to us, not by imagining their terrifying roar when all around us is quiet.

We can do this if we make that commitment.

No one ever drowned in sweat.

5

Bottoms Up

The world is a tragedy to those who feel but a comedy to those who think. —Horace Walpole

EI theory merges three primary perspectives that influence whole-person wellness; biological, cognitive (thought and perception), and social learning affects human life and emotional expression. Referenced as the *biopsychosocial* (BPS) theory, it proposes the body, mind, and environment impact the whole person.

The BPS model suggests that no single factor of human functioning exists in isolation. No particular diagnosis is sufficient to describe overall health or illness. The deep interrelation of human biology, psychology, and social learning forecasts emotional and physical health status.

EI practitioners are encouraged to view themselves and others as whole persons comprising interrelated dimensions rather than parts and pieces to be examined separately, e.g., the mind and the body operate together and are not independent of each other. Likewise, a person cannot be bad or good, an angel or a devil, or perfect or rotten to the core. We are encouraged to view ourselves and others as works in progress judged against the behavior rather than the embodiment of the whole person.

The biological precepts of EI are derivatives of established science. Without contrary proof, we cannot rationally dispute the science of human anatomy, e.g., the connection between the limbic system and emotional expression, hormones, neurons, and human operational outgrowth.

Emotional intelligence theory endorses a *bottom-up* approach to emotional problem-solving where we learn not to rely on the head (psychological) but focus on the body (biological) first to manage emotional hardship. Instead, we concentrate on eliminating the stress hormones we pump into our bodies when imagining irrational, Fearful futures or past events. The EI practitioner (you) employs an integrative, holistic treatment approach in which the biological, psychological, and social learning factors are considered. We start with the body's response to thought and work upward. We include the individual's mental and emotional needs, as well as their beliefs, values, and social context. The practitioner uses all available evidence to understand and treat presenting problems and considers various factors such as strengths, past experiences, and current situations. The practitioner understands and confronts the thoughts that initiated the body's response to Fear and develop insight and self-awareness. This approach encourages the individual to work to overcome current challenges, increase emotional flexibility, and build emotional resilience.

The term bottom-up explains the general areas of the body where emotional management must begin, using EI theory—from the toes to the head. When we make ourselves afraid, i.e., angry, depressed, jealous, frustrated, etc., we produce stress hormones and send them into our bloodstream. Stressful thinking diverts energy to the more primal part of your brain and prevents the mind from engaging in rational thought. Bottom-up stress management means employing techniques to calm the body, dissipate the stress hormones, and return to homeostasis. We will discuss some of these techniques in later chapters.

Thinking always comes second in EI theory. The body and its receptiveness to irrational thought come first. For example, let's suppose we are being ridiculed or criticized. We often believe that what we are experiencing is terrible and that we must protect ourselves from what is happening. That thought causes the body to respond defensively, sending stress hormones into the bloodstream. Because these hormones prevent rational thought and reasonable behavior, managing the physical body is our primary goal.

Our first response to terrifying thought is to mobilize the fight-flight-freeze (F^3) hormonal system. The body's memories of danger, supercharged by the brain's Fear center (part of the limbic system), take precedence over thinking things through calmly. In this state, we cannot override the primal brain's reaction without first initiating body (F^3) management.

We induce the automatic response when faced with a real or imagined threat making the stress hormones in our bloodstream the primary focus for relief. Bottom-up strategies mean we first attempt to manage the body, minimizing or eliminating the stress hormones, leading to a more collective mind and rational thought.

We do not encounter many real threats to our lives in our modern world. We principally imagine our dangers. We think, *What if this happened? What if that happened? What if I lost this? What if I had to do that?* and initiate the F^3 response where there is genuinely no need for it.

Our human design does not overthink when a mountain lion has a bead on us. Deep thought and sensitivity are not even physically possible under these conditions. Criticism, mockery, and ridicule are not life-threatening unless we believe they are. Our first thought, however, is to defend ourselves or run. Once we manage our body, EI encourages a *second thought* to organize a more sensible, balanced, and prudent outcome for this and any other event.

Although managing from the toes to the head is not often the first option for most of us, it is a strategy for reframing the aftermath of an event. Later, when we reimagine the event, we move away from the head and into the body, relaxing our breathing and muscles, patiently diminishing our body's response to its memory, settling like a shaken snow globe.

Top-down approaches, which are more typical, focus on thinking and changing thought. EI proposes that when the brain perceives danger, it is not likely to provide rational solutions. When engaged in a Fear response derived from imagination, we must manage the stress hormones shooting through our body before using our heads for problem-solving.

The bottom-up approach begins with information acquired from the body's sensations. The body's automatic response is activated because we believe we are unsafe. This life-saving response to threat is dysregulated, activated by Fearful thoughts such as losing a job, failing a test, or arguing with a cashier about a return.

When we terrorize ourselves with an imagined threat, we circulate stress hormones through our bloodstream and into vital organs, i.e., the heart, lungs, kidneys, gut, etc. These hormones include glucagon, epinephrine (adrenaline), norepinephrine, cortisol, and growth hormone, fueling the F^3.

Our goal with bottom-up stress management is to encourage the production of hormones that counter the stress response, i.e., serotonin, dopamine, GABA, and oxytocin. We can release these *feel-good* hormones using counterintuitive breathing, smiling, muscle clenching, and yawning to balance our bodies during imagined threats of harm and danger.

Bottom-up modalities incorporate dual awareness-thinking and the body's response to it. Bottom-up modalities integrate the experience of Fear, recruiting the whole person to manage stress rather than relying only on the head to address the perception of threat. Thinking in such situations is not the body's primary motivation.

The bottom-up approach recognizes that the primal part of the brain cannot act as our first source of information when we believe we are in danger. The F^3 response propels us forward even before we know it. The bottom-up approach allows for rebalancing and homeostasis and the opportunity, once relaxed, to explore solutions to our Fearful thoughts. Achieving safety and stability within the body allows for better problem-solving and emotional management.

We can develop the dual awareness of managing the body first, and then the mind can bring better improvement opportunities for emotional intelligence. Resourcing a bottom-up approach can make us feel safe where we once believed unsafe. Relieved of the stress hormones that prevent rational thinking, the mind and body can explore solutions using EI-prescribed strategies for logical reasoning.

We are like a shaken snow globe when we are in F^3 or stressed, depressed, or hopeless. The snow globe offers a clear vision of what's inside—shaking the glass globe and dispersing its glitter, fogging the once clear world within, making it harder to focus on what's inside.

It may take a minute or two of quiet to settle and regain its composed interior. But if we shake it again, we will have endless confusion inside. Stress is similar to shaking the snow globe repeatedly, never providing it with an opportunity to be still and at rest.

The same principle applies when we initiate the hormonal flushing associated with thinking something Fearful when it isn't threatening our safety. As thought activates the stress response, releasing adrenaline and other substances into the body, the mind will not stop swirling if we repeatedly think the same miserable, frightening thoughts. Like shaking a snow globe, we must learn to be patient and relax while waiting for gravity to do its magic.

You cannot use a nutty head to manage a nutty head. That strategy will result in more nutty thoughts leading to even nuttier behaviors. Managing the hormones spinning like glitter in our minds and bodies is essential for regaining homeostasis and balance and ultimately making rational thinking more possible. We will learn more about bottom-up emotional management techniques in the following chapters.

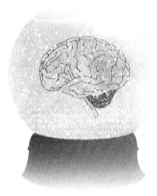

The brain's FearNot (R^3) center, or the *parasympathetic* response, is the biological opposite of the Fear center (F^3), the *sympathetic* system. This response is the rest, digest, and repair system. When parasympathetic activity dominates, healing and regeneration occur. In this state, the brain and body perform activities in harmony necessary for digestion, detoxification, elimination, and building immunity.

R^3 represents perception and thought that provide balance and a sense of well-being. Biochemically, we replace adrenaline and cortisol, the stress hormones generated during F^3, with the R^3 opposites. In the R^3 state, we may feel lethargic because our bodies are in repair mode slowing the heart and breathing rates, lowering blood pressure, and promoting digestion. Our body enters a state of relaxation, supporting recovery.

We are often engulfed in F^3 biochemicals in a split second. All we have to do is think of something alarming, have an argument, feel threatened, or ingest too much alcohol, caffeine, or cigarettes. Bringing about parasympathetic activity takes more time than bringing on the F^3 response. To get into healing mode, we must first manage the body and the biochemicals produced from the F^3 reaction, then engage the mind in more rational decision-making. For some people, mindful meditation may help, while others may be quietly in motion, walking in Nature, or swimming. When seeking to go from the F^3 to the R^3 states, the most important goal is that body management must come first.

It may seem counterintuitive to change your thought cycle to focus on your breathing and muscles to manage what you believe to be your emotional problems. When we are in a Fear state, the body only trusts messages from the body. Thinking must wait for the body to calm itself. Only then can we respond to the circumstances we face with rational thought.

Depending on age, temperament, genetics, and training, you will learn to think twice (in place of the urgent, single thought most of us use in times of disturbance and rarely alter) as a system of EI improvement. After using body management techniques, the goal is to change our self-talk, asking, "What am I afraid of," and seeking an answer, thereby thinking of something new and more adaptive. Rather than endlessly cycling self-destructive, Fearful thinking, we must endeavor to move our thoughts to manage our body and its initial chemical response to our Fearful view.

Nature cannot give you a spurt of relaxation like it can give you a spurt of urgency. If stress mode has been your preferred way of being, you may have to make a conscious effort to slow it down. When we tell ourselves we are in danger, real or imagined, adrenaline consistently outperforms serenity's chemistry.

Over time, too much F^3 dominance can lead to the inability to absorb nutrients from food, overweight, poor blood sugar regulation, depression, learning issues, chronic exhaustion, insomnia, aches and pains, and ultimately severe illnesses like diabetes. These are the logical result of calling on the glands for one emergency after another, whether the emergency is real or imagined.

The practice of psychology traditionally supports the theory that human emotion is directly related to thought and perception. We feel because we think. Therefore, the best, most efficient method for changing how you feel is to make an effort to change how you think. This theory is only partially true, and there is something much more profound at work.

We are becoming more aware that the older, more instinctual part of your brain (the limbic system) has superiority over your cortex. There is little we can do intellectually to override the nervous system when in a Fear state. We must first focus on the body, and the impact thought has on the body rather than immediately attempting to change the view that instigated it.

Most of us cannot rely on changing our thoughts as the primary method for improving emotional expression. When we think nervously and Fearfully, whether the impending threat is real or imagined, the nervous system must be the primary focus of our attention. When we can clear the stress hormones, we expel thought into our bloodstream, and we are more likely to use reason to solve problems. Better navigation into the body's response to the idea and the parts of the activated nervous system can help improve emotional intelligence.

Nature had hoped that humans would benefit from a brain system uniquely designed to protect us from real threats, aiding in the process of quickly, effortlessly climbing trees and making ourselves safe in the limbs to continue for another day with our primary goals of eating, sleeping, socializing, and ultimately making babies. In those days, about 175,000 years ago, when our limbic system resembled the one we have now, we came down from the trees. We engaged the opposite parts of our brains, regained balance, and resumed our living activities on the ground.

Modern humankind spends the day in the trees, afraid to come down, having no way to control the imagination that keeps them there. Because we use our vision of the past and the future to construct our Fears, there is no end to the possibilities of danger. So we have returned to the treetops, ordering in, socializing online, working from home, and sedating our stress response using less prosocial, maladaptive, and addictive habits. I usually have this discussion with those who venture into my office for help with F^3:

"I hope you don't think I'm being dismissive, but your problems seem entirely imaginary."

"Imaginary? What do you mean by imaginary? My problems are real."

"Well," I say, "the evidence that you are safe, well-nourished, well-hydrated, and in no danger sits before me." I often pause to gauge acceptance of this incredible view. "Tell me what you have to Fear if you do not use the future or the past to describe your Fears."

"I have to make plans, don't I? If I didn't, I'd just, well, anything is possible!"

"I think it may be best to make flexible plans and never forget that no matter what happens next, you will handle it as you have handled everything in your life so far."

"There are things in my past I haven't handled."

"I promise you; you've handled everything in your past already. You can't handle it again. It may help to stop trying and accept there is nothing you can do about your past."

"I have to prepare."

"Prepare for the future *flexibly*."

"What will I do in the meantime?"

"When there is nothing you can do, do nothing."

"That's a scary idea."

"That's because you're imagining the future."

It is more likely that the imagination, particularly the image of what will happen, instead of what is happening, instigates the F^3 response, sustains it in overdrive, and keeps us sitting in trees.

A healthy nervous system quickly alternates between these two states, preferring to spend more time calm than in overdrive. This preference contributes to the urgency we put into taking care of problems before they happen, instigating the opposite response and inducing the opposite result.

Our nervous system goes through a natural cycle of being at rest and then alert, possibly in the F^3 response or some performance level, shuddering, returning to R^3, resting, and digesting.

Peter Levine, the creator of somatic experiencing therapy, uses the example of a polar bear to demonstrate the nervous system cycle. He describes a polar bear in the wild peacefully going about business when a group of researchers in a helicopter chase him down and shoot him with a tranquilizer dart. The bear cannot stop the researchers from examining it and tagging it. After the researchers leave, the bear begins to shake violently, his body's natural response to trauma, burning off the excess adrenaline that surged through his body when he was trapped and lingered in its bloodstream. After shaking, the bear walks away with no leftover effects from its experience. The bear returns to a calm state, hunting and eating as he did before the attack.

The cycle from the R^3 to the F^3 to the R^3 response is the essence of standard emotional processing in our human body. We start with a resting state, go on the alert then shake it off. Humans often readjust by laughing or physically shaking or crying and eventually feel safe again. It may be more difficult for people to use these skills when their imagination tells them they face danger. Committing to performing these counterintuitive behaviors is the first step in EI emotional management.

The insight offered by the bear's story may lie in the shake-it-off behavior. People may shake, even flapping their cheeks from side to side, to regain emotional balance if they hear something horrible or ugly. If we discuss an event where someone mainly lies, they may respond by shaking their head and shoulders vigorously. Sometimes we react by laughing, pushing air out of our lungs, and crying simultaneously. These behaviors are your body trying to burn off adrenaline and process the stress chemicals that flood the body. The body naturally tries to return to calm using physical activity.

Humans have enormous, complex brains compared to other animals. Our cortex, the thinking part of the brain, helps us plan things out, think things through, and have self-control. But our brains can work against us, imploring us not to cry and declaring that *I cannot stand this!* Or act as if nothing is happening. We tell ourselves not to shake, not to think, or not to show Fear. Our brilliant mind works to avoid the raw, visceral physical response to thought by inferring that we are safer by not showing how we think and feel. Our bodies hold the deep wisdom of knowing when and how to express emotion. Our natural ability to resolve emotional conflict often restricts it, trapping how we feel inside our body and brain, leaving it unexpressed, trapped in muscle, bone, and blood, producing free-floating F^3, stress chemicals, and hormones like cortisol with no informed way of managing them.

We might emphasize that emotional intelligence theory proposes that a person cannot have only one disease. This description may stand as an incomplete path toward a fuller understanding.

Once the expressions of grief, Fear, and shame occur honestly, without restriction, and with vigorous physical manifestation, we can expect to regain homeostasis. We can learn to breathe deeply, smile, walk it out, and practice mindfulness when in a state of Fear.

Likewise, there are signs of how we claim balance in our daily activities. A cat's purr can lower stress, help with difficult breathing, lower blood pressure, heal infections, and even heal bones. Dogs will yawn to show such things as submissiveness and to manage Fear. Other animals will shake, like the bear, after an aggressive encounter with another animal. Most animals will sigh or whine to express distress.

Can we precisely, empirically say that our trauma stores in our shoulders, back, hips, or feet? No, because we don't have the tools to measure that. We can confidently say, however, that physical activity is often robust at resetting the nervous system and healing F^3 and trauma. So if you're complaining of stress or even post-traumatic memories, you may try these to engage in activities related to activating the R^3 response when the F^3 is in full effect.

I believe in evidence-based treatments, which have been shown through rigorous research to be effective consistently and not harmful in treating these disorders. I am not a proponent of energy healing, rebirthing, crystals, or chakra balancing, and many alternative emotional management treatments might sell more than the research can back up. Still, the anecdotal evidence is that people experience something other than what they felt before the experience. So, if it works, do more of it.

People claim that body-based modality work for them, and the research is starting to catch up with the benefits of physical treatments as an effective way to treat stress. Biological therapies like acupressure, massage, dancing, or deep belly breathing, are all things that people say help them focus and rebalance the nervous system. Exercise is thought to be more effective than medication at treating mild to moderate depression and F^3, assisting the nervous system through natural activation and relaxation cycles.

Chronic stress is the thermostat getting turned up, activating the fight-flight-freeze response, making it very sensitive to specific thoughts. When we train it to turn on quickly, it stays on; this way, stress may get held in the mind and body even when we may not consciously think about a particular event. An unhealthy nervous system gets stuck in elevated stress levels, rarely going through cycles of calm.

When the sympathetic nervous system takes over, we feel constantly anxious, in danger at the slightest signal, and find it very difficult to relax. We experience periodic exhaustion, crashing, and a complete loss of energy in these states. We're often unaware of how we're going into high alert mode, which leads to us being trapped in it even longer.

It's not healthy to be on high alert all day and then collapse at home, watching TV and eating to relax and recharge. We can learn to regulate our nervous system throughout the day. We are often stuck in an F^3 state, exhausted, traumatized, and burnt out. In that case, we can build a healthy nervous system through relaxed vigilance, learning to trigger the parasympathetic response, that calming response in your nervous system, in small amounts, throughout the day, by doing simple body-based exercises. We can learn to take deep breaths or tense and soften muscle groups, building a parasympathetically dominant nervous system.

With practice throughout the day, you can train yourself to be more self-aware and mindful of your opportunities for relaxation.

It may take some practice.

No one ever drowned in sweat.

6

Stay On Your Toes

"The art of love is largely the art of persistence."—
Albert Ellis

We can use many simple breathing techniques to help relieve stress and activate the R^3 system. The military uses one breathing technique with Special Operations deployed on missions requiring exceptional self-control and emotional management, particularly the F^3 response. The method is called *box breathing* or *square breathing*.

BOX BREATHING

A deep breathing technique that can help you slow down your breathing to deactivate the F^3 response and activate the R^3 response. It works by distracting your mind (mindfulness) as you count, tracing an imaginary box with your mind, calming your nervous system, and decreasing stress in your body. We can use this technique anywhere and anytime, but we often use it when our F^3 is overactivated, aiding whole-body management and overall wellness.

1. Imagine the shape of a box. You can close your eyes or leave them open, staring into the air at nothing in particular.

2. Breathe into your lungs deeply for four seconds.

3. Imagine tracing the box with your mind, going up one side of the square.

4. Hold your breath for four seconds.

5. Move to the second wall and exhale through your pursed lips for four seconds. (Shape your lips as if you were blowing through a straw.)

6. Move to the third wall of the square and inhale deeply for four seconds.

7. Move to the fourth wall and exhale through pursed lips for four seconds.

8. If you feel dizzy, change how deeply you inhale, how long you hold your breath, and how long you exhale.

9. Repeat this process, concentrating on your imagination of the square and your breathing. Think only of the imagined square and the pace, depth, and fullness of your breathing.

10. Shake your shoulders and head when you feel that you are sufficiently relaxed.

11. Repeat as needed.

DIAPHRAGMATIC BREATHING

Our next breathing skill will use our tight pursed lips with belly or diaphragmatic breathing. Pursed lips cause the lungs to work harder when the exhale opening is smaller. Belly breathing, or diaphragmatic breathing, is the skill of breathing through your belly instead of through your chest.

There are various forms of diaphragmatic breathing. Essential diaphragmatic breathing is the simplest form. To perform basic diaphragmatic breathing, follow the instructions below:

1. Lie on a flat surface with a pillow under the head and pillows beneath the knees. Pillows will help keep the body in a comfortable position.
2. Place one hand on the middle of the upper chest.
3. Place the other hand on the stomach, beneath the rib cage but above the diaphragm.
4. Slowly breathe through the nose to inhale, drawing the breath toward the stomach. The stomach should push upward against the hand while the chest remains still.
5. To exhale, tighten the abdominal muscles and let the stomach fall downward while exhaling through pursed lips. Again, the chest should remain still.

It would help if you practiced this breathing exercise for 5–10 minutes, three to four times daily. Once you become comfortable with diaphragmatic breathing, you may start to practice while seated or standing. When practicing diaphragmatic breathing in these positions, it is crucial to keep the shoulders, head, and neck relaxed.

SMILING

Studies have shown that *smiling* releases endorphins, other natural painkillers, and serotonin helping to deactivate the F^3 response and activate the R^3 response. These brain chemicals make us feel good from head to toe, elevate our mood, relax our bodies, and reduce physical pain. This exercise is counterintuitive. It's often difficult to move your lips and face in this way when you believe you are facing catastrophe. Use this technique when you think of something unpleasant, remember something from the past (not reliving but instead revisiting), or experience something distasteful, use this technique. I promise it won't be easy:

1. Smile broadly.

2. Move your cheeks up as far as possible.

3. Lower.

4. Repeat.

Smiling releases helps us feel more hopeful, resilient, and upbeat. Smiling can have the same effect on those around us who observe us using this technique. Facial expressions can improve our mood and increase more adaptive thoughts. Smiling also allows the body to adapt, moving from the F^3 response to the R^3 state of rest, relaxation, and resuming life. A smile spurs a chemical reaction in the brain, releasing certain hormones, including dopamine and serotonin. Dopamine increases our feelings of happiness, and Serotonin release is associated with reduced stress. You may have to do it repeatedly, possibly for two or three minutes, but in no time, the long-term benefits are more significant than the short time you use the skill.

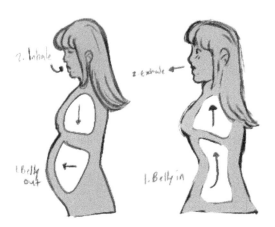

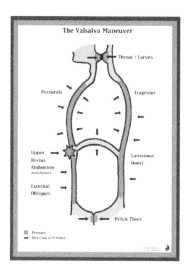

THE VALSALVA MANEUVER

The *Valsalva maneuver* is a breathing method that may slow your heart when beating too fast. This activity creates a forceful strain that can trigger your heart to react and return to a normal rhythm. We often use the Valsalva maneuver to unclog ears, but it can also restore homeostasis and the R^3 response. We recommend this skill when an individual is experiencing higher-than-average episodes of stress.

To perform the Valsalva maneuver, you should close your mouth, pinch your nose shut and press the air like you are blowing up a balloon. You can also use the Valsalva maneuver by imagining that you are squatting to lift a heavy weight or how you would push if you were having trouble moving your bowels. We do not recommend using this technique more than once in four or five minutes. We shouldn't use the Valsalva maneuver if we have cardiovascular problems. Don't try this technique if you have high blood pressure and are at increased risk of stroke or heart attack. Talk to your doctor before trying this technique if you have a heart rhythm problem, also known as an arrhythmia.

MINDFUL BREATHING

Finally, my favorite, *mindful breathing*, can do wonders as we build a parasympathetically dominant nervous system. We can do mindful breathing exercises anywhere, anytime, which is the optimal recipe for R^3 living. Conscious breathing is a fundamental yet powerful meditation practice. The idea is to focus on your breathing, its natural rhythm, flow, and how it feels on each inhale and exhale.

Focusing on the breath is particularly helpful because it serves as an anchor—something you can turn your attention to at any time if you feel stressed or carried away by negative thinking, activating the F^3 response. The fact is, our brains can only think of one thing at a time. We do think rapidly, causing us to think we are doing more than one thing at a time, but it's only one but very, very quickly. We can take advantage of that fact to control our past and future thoughts and bring them into the moment.

Of course, our minds love to wonder about the expanse of our imagination. Our human design predicts that behavior. There was a time long ago when we had to use our skills to reimagine the past and imagine the future to stay alive. It was essential to know where the buffalo roamed the years before and where we sleep when the sun goes down. Most of us no longer have to do that. But our minds are wired to do it anyway. So when we practice mindful breathing, we may notice our frisky minds looking for something else to do. In that case, we can be curious about our minds and coax, ease, and invite them back to the moment. This cajoling is a precarious place to manage. Suppose we demand that our mind come back to the exercise. In that case, we will activate the F^3 response and flood our nervous system with stress hormones, defeating the purpose of what we are hoping to accomplish.

"How are you doing with your mindful breathing goal?"

"I'm *trying* to do it, but when I do it, I think about what I'm going to do when I finish."

"You are not supposed to *try* to meditate; you *just are* meditating. You *are* already, and meditation isn't an attempt at being or doing. If you *try* to meditate, you will create a stress response."

"Yeah, I noticed that. When I get done, I'm usually a mess. I use an egg timer. Is there anything else I can do? Something that doesn't take as much concentration. I have ADHD, you know."

Close your eyes and rest your hands on your knees. Bring your attention to the touch of your body on your seat. Feel the weight of your body on your chair or cushion. Make sure that your back is straight and that you're comfortable. Take a few deep breaths. While deep breathing, relax your shoulders and your stomach muscles, the muscles in your face, hands, and legs. Let go of all the tightness in your body. Bring your attention back to your breath. Notice what it feels like as it enters through your nose, goes down through your throat, fills your lungs, and back out through your nose. Notice your stomach and chest rise and fall each time you breathe in and each time you breathe out. Just allow your breathing to be natural and relaxed. Bring your attention to the feeling of your breath in your nose. Feel your breath as it comes in and goes out. Notice his sensation. Notice your breathing each time you breathe out. As you inhale, your breath feels cool. As you exhale, it feels warmer. When your mind wanders or you become distracted, notice what's going on in your head and gently bring your attention back to your breath going in and out. Notice the feeling of your breath and allow your thoughts and feelings to come and go. Gently bring your mind back to the touch of your body on our seat and open your eyes.

Our nervous system has a fantastic ability to change and grow depending on how we use it. Promising research shows that we can change the physical structure, the chemical balance, and the electrical activity in our brain depending on how we use it. We can even influence our genes and how they're activated and passed on. We can learn to have quite a bit of influence on our nervous system, training it to start when we need to wake up, perform tasks, or respond to problems and teaching it to calm down when it's time to relax, recoup, process, or to repair, and do it through physical, emotional, and psychological exercises.

We can make more intentional and powerful life choices when we're calm within. We create calm by resolving the needs of survival and attachment and training our brains to feel safe.

We can grow a pear where there was once only an apple.

It will take the force of will to do that.

No one ever drowned in sweat.

7

Use Your Inside Voice

You have been the last dream of my soul.
—Charles Dickens, *A Tale of Two Cities*

Little is as important to human life as the quality and consequence of emotion. Emotion can promote hope, dampen optimism, and weaken and strengthen human connections, sometimes with as little as a twitch of an eye or the flick of a finger.

In the early 19th century, Scottish philosopher Thomas Brown introduced the word *emotion* to the English language. Before then, we described mental states as *appetites, passions, affections,* or *sentiments* with primary emphasis placed on bearing, comportment, or the manner through which we expressed our feelings.

The word emotion has its roots in the French word *émotion,* meaning a physical disturbance. The word and the concept of emotion came into much broader use in 18th century English, often to refer to mental experiences. Emotion became a fully-fledged theoretical term in the following century, inseparable from *feeling* and *mood*. The word emotion and its curiosity as a thingamajig is a new idea, ever in flux and never quite fully defined.

EI defines emotion as a phenomenon of thought and perception. These two cognitive processes transform into behavior, leaving emotional management a system of thought modification. Essentially, if we think something, we will derive an emotional consequence. With that in mind, altering emotion would logically require modifying thought.

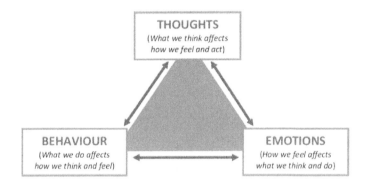

If we hope to modify our emotional state, we must first know our minds, their genetic origins, and their influence on our physical functioning. EI begins with awareness of the inner nature of things or improving our interpretations of events using a better-quality inside voice or self-talk.

Self-talk is how you talk inside your head. Your mind is never without a thought, so listen for it. Your inside voice draws from beliefs—the shoulds, the oughts, the musts, the have-tos, and the needs you accumulate over a lifetime. These are the words you use to determine your perception of everything. Improvement in EI depends on knowing this inner voice—the internal monologue you use throughout the day.

Behavior change is complex because it requires a person to disrupt a current habit while fostering a new, possibly unfamiliar, set of actions. Better-quality self-talk is no different; it takes time to revise how we've learned to think and behave—usually longer than we prefer to spend on it.

Taking a pill to achieve this result is always a more attractive alternative. Medications, however, lead only to postponing the inevitable. Whenever you are having an emotional hardship, taking a pill prevents skill-building and durability for the next time something similar happens. If you use a drug to manage your trouble, you will seek medication the next time you have a problem. If we engage with our issues and build skills in handling them, we will be stronger and more adept the next time we encounter a challenge. Hard work and concentrated effort are the answers to driven emotional wellness. We can never sideline the value of effort and ownership for something more manageable. When our emotional perspective is under our influence, it will provide a more worthwhile outcome.

The early Stoics believed in logos (the Greek term for *word*), introduced by Heraclitus about five hundred B.C.E., to indicate his conception of language (spoken and internal) as the universal force of reason governing everything. In the same way, our internal language or self-talk binds ideas to experiences by shaping sensory information.

Apart from its purposes for emotional expression, we use language to understand ourselves and our motivations, set our goals, and interpret the results of our efforts. Language is also the primary way of deciding the nature and extent of emotional wellness in ourselves and others.

People tend to talk and think about what is most important to them. We talk about our values, beliefs, pasts, and futures. The words *average* and *abnormal* form a large part of our opinion of ourselves—how much are we like others and how much is not. These concepts contribute to our conceptualization of ourselves and can be an additional source of examined self-talk.

Experience can shape psychology; EI considers the experience of repetitive thinking patterns on the expression of emotion. EI believes the past contributes to emotional expression but is not the best resource for present-moment emotional management. Our primary resource for emotional information is our thinking or self-talk, our internal dialogue, or how we speak to ourselves.

Our inner language is the product of repeated experiences across our lifespan. We begin to separate knowledge derived from experience from the start of life into categories representing *meaning*. Meaning is subjective and limited by personal perspectives or preferences. In contrast, a broader analysis of an event or circumstance can influence meaning and help create a more comprehensive set of options for emotional expression. For example, "I lost my job, and that is a disaster!" versus "I lost my job, and that is a manageable inconvenience and possibly an opportunity."

No situation or circumstance holds inherent meaning. All events require interpretation to acquire worth. The meaning we apply to the conditions and circumstances we encounter motivates the body's sensations and responses to the event. Our body will respond according to our thoughts if we use a catastrophic definition to define a problem. Likewise, applying a more reasonable interpretation of any event will help manage our body's response to it.

Self-talk plays a fundamental role in expressing emotion, helping us use acquired knowledge to make meaning of repeated sensory perceptions. Self-talk is the glue for emotional expression, binding concepts to a physical response and shaping sensory information.

Anticipatory (future) and retrospective (past) thinking are the principal sources of damaging emotions. EI considers mindful awareness integral for managing overall health.

While human biology, particularly the parasympathetic nervous system, is fundamental to conceptualizing human emotion, EI theory does not emphasize recalling the past to understand the mind in the present moment. Remembering the past relies on imagination to define our response to it. Regardless of its consequence, the past and its imaginative derivative cannot represent its uniqueness.

Our past likely shapes our minds, but it does not shape the singular richness of the present moment; there must be some level of willing cooperation for engaging in memory and formulating a newer, more adaptive response. What we tell ourselves about our past in the present moment holds far more therapeutic value than recalling it and asking, "Why?" For example, we may describe ourselves unable to form intimate relationships because of early-stage childhood trauma. The elegant application of the psychodynamic model may encourage the individual who asks why to represent the past events of their lives in detail from memory. We identify the *why,* working from that frame of reference. Regardless of how far back we can reimagine, we eventually return to the present moment, where our thoughts about the past have always been. EI suggests that we begin our discussion of the present moment and our thoughts at the moment rather than spending precious time telling stories about things we cannot change. We cannot change the past, but we can change how we think about our personal history in the present.

"Now that we've relived your past, what can we do about it?"

"Do about it? It's a terrible, tangled mess. I cannot live with these memories. They memories are destroying me."

"What does all this catastrophe mean about you now?"

"It means *I'm in pieces*. I will never be complete."

"Let's talk about that."

"Talk about what?"

"I want you to prove you're not good enough because you've had unpleasant experiences."

The EI approach may ask the individual to describe some event from the past, not asking *why* but *how* that event influences the present moment. EI attempts to bring the individual into the present moment, to live *with the moment*, recognizing that past thoughts are neither reliable nor helpful in achieving a more manageable mind frame.

"I just want to know why."

"Crap happens."

"Why me?"

"Why not you?"

"Why do I feel so defeated?"

"How do you make yourself feel that way?"

"I think about all this crap."

"Why don't we explore what you're telling yourself about the past? Let's find out how you are resurrecting the past, looking for answers to why. You could spend our time learning how you make yourself feel the way you do."

We cannot alter in any way the events of our past. We can change our thoughts about the past, the inner dialogue we incessantly use to remind ourselves of our past, and how we use that inaccurate, often self-destructive, and maladaptive information to predict the future as a disaster.

Self-destructive behavior results from unnecessary harm by putting ourselves in harmful situations, *disturbing* ourselves, or keeping ourselves from solutions because we believe the past is the best predictor of the future. As appealing as it is in a meme, the past does not predict the future. Every moment is unique, and we can engage with it more hopefully, rationally, and self-approvingly.

EI theory's goal is to acknowledge the past, leading to full acceptance of it. Claiming acceptance of the past, regardless of its horrors, is not to *like* the past. (You can accept what you don't like.) Acceptance recognizes the limitations of changing the past and living contentedly with the present moment. EI theory emphasizes that it is not as helpful to know *why* we feel as we do but understand *how* we re-disturb ourselves about the past in the present moment using self-talk.

Additionally, EI theory emphasizes the influence of self-talk on whole-body wellness. The F^3 is the biochemical reaction both humans and animals experience during intense stress or Fear, whether real or *imagined*. For instance, if a bear wandered into your room at this very moment, you would likely feel the heat of the F^3 response burst through your body. However, it would not be the bear that would set off the body's internal security alarm; instead, it would be your imagination of what the bear *could* or *would* do rather than what it is doing.

Self-talk can activate the sympathetic nervous system by sending messages to the brain to initiate a response in the body. The hypothalamus activates the adrenal cortical system. This structure uses the bloodstream to carry its urgent messages, providing the body with energy to respond to real and imagined dangers. A surge of adrenaline helps handle the threat by increasing the heart rate and blood pressure, rendering the entire body hyper-alert.

Of course, running from a bear, a lion, or even a garden snake is the best, most resourceful use of the F^3 response. However, we often imagine job loss, traffic jams, disrespect, or contracting a disease as actual dangers and, by doing so, activate the Fear system.

If we can imagine it, our brains will cooperate.

Likewise, if you imagine biting into a thick, juicy yellow lemon wedge, your salivary glands will gladly collaborate with your thoughts and produce a sour sensation on your tongue.

Conceptualizing self-talk as an instigator of the interplay between biological, psychological, and social learning domains can improve emotional intelligence.

Finally, EI improvement is a lifestyle; it is not an issue-specific therapy type. Improvement results from what we repeatedly do to increase awareness of ourselves and others. Interest and insight motivate EI improvement. Interest is an affection for something, an enduring predisposition to reengage over time. Insight using EI can be derived from the attention we pay to our self-talk.

When we welcome these two ideas into our daily lives, we can promote a lifelong interest in improving emotional intelligence.

No one ever drowned in sweat.

8

The Moth

*To be yourself in a world that is constantly trying to make you
something else is the greatest accomplishment.*
— Ralph Waldo Emerson

Introspection is the examination or observation of one's own mental and emotional processes. Self-reflection is the act of thinking about one's own thoughts, feelings, and actions. Both introspection and self-reflection involve considering one's own inner experiences and can be used for personal growth and self-improvement.

Introspection and self-reflection involve looking inward to examine one's thoughts and motivations—exploring thinking, often resulting in better emotional insight. We can use this technique to identify opportunities for gratitude self-and-other acceptance and satisfy our curiosity about how we think and operate. Once recalled, using introspection and reflection techniques, we can engage in events from the past to understand their meaning and the feelings we have toward them.

Introspection and reflection allow us to audit how we process our memories and how they may have become a part of our subconscious thought. By this, we may appreciate the value of our experiences from a distance, as if observing ourselves from above. Motives for introspection and reflection are everywhere. Prepare for them and accept them when they present themselves.

We often overlook these special occasions.

One of the more meaningful experiences I had with introspection and self-analysis involved a woman who visited my office several years ago. "Goodness," I said, "You scared me." I paused in the reception window, not expecting to see her sitting in the chair. I knew who was next on my schedule, and it was not the woman in the waiting room.

She would have been undetectable if not for her perfume and the sound of the cellophane she removed from her peppermint candy. The corners of her eyes rose sharply from behind her powder blue surgical mask, letting me know she was smiling in this new age of COVID-19. She lifted the mask and placed the mint on her tongue. She pulled her cell phone from her coat pocket. She held it up, revealing a text reminder she had received. She said, "I've been waiting almost two weeks." She swallowed her minty saliva. "How long will our session be?"

I had taken the sign-in sheets and other germy things out of my reception as a precaution against transferring the virus. No pens, no paper, no pamphlets. Only a simple human greeting and a highly specialized, computerized check-in. "About an hour," I said, "I'll be with you." I sat in the chair behind the computer and checked my schedule for clues about the woman's identity. (The disadvantage of the CDC-prescribed procedures for checking in patients was that I couldn't slyly look at the patient registration login to know the person's name, leaving the illusion that I had remembered them on my own.)

As I searched for the woman on my computer, I had no idea who she was. A younger man entered through the glass door and greeted me with a familiar hand wave. His mask muffled his greeting, but I detected his smile by the creases on his forehead. He sat down, and I realized I had not synched my schedule with the reality unfolding before me.

I smiled and said, "I think we have a problem. Unless you two are together." They both laughed softly. I searched for creases in their foreheads that meant they were comfortable. I said, "I'm sorry. Mix-ups happen now and then. Give me a minute." I tapped some keys on the keyboard and looked for some explanation. The woman and the young man watched, seemingly unsure what I would do to solve the problem.

Who would stay, and who would go?

Who would I sacrifice?

I was faced with *Sophie's Choice*, waiting for the perfect moment to say, "Can you come back in an hour?" I directed my masked face at the boy and away from the mysterious, older woman.

"Sure," he said, standing and reaching for his cell phone as if out of reflex. "I'll just go around the corner to Shake Shack." He pulled open the door. "Can I get you something?" he asked the woman.

"No, thank you so much," she said, her tone perfectly balancing that I had chosen her over him, careful not to show happiness at his expense.

Although it was the middle of summer in Las Vegas, nearly 110°, the woman wore a heavy, black woolen coat. With the first deathly wave of COVID-19, I had become accustomed to seeing people wearing original protective clothing to avoid contamination from the virus. Most wore blue paper masks over their face and nose, but some wore them only over their mouths. Others let them hang below their chins. Some sewed more fashionable covers, symbols painted on, cartoonish mouths, noses, and tongues. Some even more cautious people wear yard gloves and shop for homemade hand sanitizer ingredients—alcohol, cucumber lotion, and a dab of bleach.

I didn't ask about the woman's heavy coat. "Have a seat there," I said, pointing my finger at the chair in my therapy room, fifteen feet from where I would sit. "Can I get you something to drink?"

"Oh no," she said as if the offer was incredible under the dire circumstances. She sat, and I took my chair. I squirted some hand sanitizer onto my fingers and rubbed it into my palms and forearms. "Well, how are we today?" I asked, reaching for my Starbucks coffee. "How's the weather out there? Chilly?"

"It's pretty nice," she said, unfastening the button closest to her neck. She paused, "Why are people suddenly wearing masks on their chins? I call them chin bras?" She giggled at her joke. "People should put their masks on their faces instead of hanging down under their chins."

As the COVID-19 virus swept our nation, the government asked that people shelter in place, meaning staying at home unless it was absolutely, categorically incontestably necessary. The CDC deemed doctor's appointments essential travel, but we should remember that the virus was more likely to kill people 65 and older. The mandate to stay home was incredibly difficult for people in this vulnerable age range.

Before the outbreak, many aged Americans were already confined to their homes, having an incapacitating illness or a simple lack of funds, leaving many isolated with limited entertainment options and connections.

The virus and its seemingly daily change in rules forced aged people to avoid meeting with their friends and families and endure life in sequestration. Separated, even from strangers in the grocery store, wearing garden gloves, heavy coats, and rubber boots for Fear of getting or giving the virus, the onset of depression set in.

No longer approved to take an inexpensive stroll in a park, the hope of encountering a stray dog on the sidewalk or the pièce de resistance, striking up a conversation with a young mother who is happy to yield her responsibility for *Push me!* to a willing volunteer grandparent.

The woman settled into her chair, and I invited her to take off her mask. After all, we were seated comfortably and protectively. I imagined the CDC bestowing an award for meeting their guidelines. I noticed a moth in the window, flying into the glass, repeatedly hitting its head and fluttering its wings. My attention remained on the moth longer than I had expected, imagining it could be a COVID-19 carrier. "Oh, I'm sorry. You were saying?" I said, waking from my trance

"I wonder how that got in here," she said, "Seems odd."

We had been having a moth problem in our building since the start of the virus. I somehow associated the occasional moth with the virus. I imagined the moth's powdery wings trembling in search of an escape route, like my hopes to be free of COVID finally.

Her face was exposed. She smiled from ear to ear as if she had come up for air after submerging in murky swamp water. She gripped her purse and placed it squarely on her lap. She removed another mint from her pocket, twisted its cellophane wrapper, and set it on her tongue. "Would you like one," she asked, "I keep forgetting." She drew back her hand. "We can't touch."

My eyes returned to her face and then to the moth on the window ledge, where it sat, preparing for an embattled, wasted struggle to escape to freedom.

The woman's face spoke to me about where she had been, where she was going, and how she could influence my predictions with a sudden smile as she began telling me her story, as hundreds before her had done. She described her employment, "They sent everyone home. Most people were pretty happy about it, but I got my people-fix. I like going to work to be around people. Otherwise, I wouldn't see anyone for days and days." She described her job. "I work to stay busy," she explained, nudging me to move my lips to show empathy and understanding.

"Do you have any other income," I asked, "Social Security, perhaps? I'm not entirely sure how Social Security works, but you might be eligible."

"I like to work," she said, "I don't like to be alone. I do get Medicare, thank Jesus. I'm starting to realize I'm probably going to work forever. I mean, what else would I do all day?"

The woman described her duties as a receptionist. She showed joy over her encounters with people from all walks of life and helped resolve quick and easy problems or directed them to the appropriate city office. "They demoted me," she said suddenly but softly. "They put me in the back room with the filing cabinets." She was left to work alone. She sighed, "I liked my job. Poof! Gone!"

As a receptionist, her income was manageable. Her demotion, however, relegated her to put paper into folders and folders into cabinets. She was isolated and reduced in pay. "I'm pretty sure they just want to get rid of me now," she said, looking at her lap. "I think they just want me to give up."

Her job was necessary to pay her bills, but she read some of the reports she filed out of boredom. "There's a lot of stuff going on in the world. Those child protection reports and domestic violence things are a nightmare. It's terrible. Every day, there's something new. It keeps me on my toes." She gripped her purse.

"People are very complicated," I said.

The woman added that she had recently lost her *best friend* of forty-three years, leaving her alone and without companionship. "Our income together was enough for a vacation or a few nights out on the town," she said. "No more of that." She motioned with her hands, "Poof!" like a magician's wand over a top hat.

"No children?" I asked, my eyes drawn back to the moth in the window. "I mean, were either of you married before you became roommates?"

The moth had restarted its endless flight, intent on making it through the glass rather than finding another way out. "What was her name?" I asked, seemingly awakening from a foggy daze. "That's a long friendship."

"Rosalyn," the woman said as if recalling the sound of footsteps on an old, creaky staircase. She seemed suddenly tense and uncomfortable. She again gripped her purse with both hands. "Roz was my best friend, and we were like this." She crossed her fingers and held them up for me to admire. "She would've gone down there when they started to mess with me—when they took my job away. Poof! She would have told them. She always knew how to straighten things out." She reached for a tissue. "Her family came from Utah and took her away the day she died. Poof! Gone!" She dabbed at her eyes with her tissue. "I'm sorry," she said.

I paused, fascinated by the woman's story, Fearful of frightening her with the questions I suddenly had about Roz and their lifelong friendship. I looked at her, hoping she would speak without asking any questions.

"Cancer," she said. "She knew all about trees. Taught me everything I know. I have her here inside my head." She pointed at her right temple. "I can still see her, one knee on the ground, smiling at me in that stupid Red Sox cap."

The woman explained how trees grow and how she and her best friend Roz would experiment, grafting limbs to contrasting hosts to determine if the limbs could mate with one another.

The woman explained fruit tree grafting as a technique used to propagate specific fruit varieties by inserting a twig or branch into the rootstock of another plant. She explained that a new branch of the transferred variety would grow if the procedure were successful. She lowered her head and explained that she felt sad when the process didn't work. "We buried the ones that didn't make it in the same pot with the roots of the host," she said. She suddenly stirred. "We grafted a pear scion to an apple rootstock!" She quickly paused. "Everyone said we couldn't do it. It stayed alive for only 17 days, and then it died. Poof!"

"I'm sorry to hear that Roz died," I said.

"Roz," she said, "I miss her terribly."

"I know you do."

The woman opened the gold clasp on her purse and removed a withered twig. "Here it is," she said, admiring the small brown branch. "This is our branch." She twirled it between her fingers and looked at me as if singing a song she had held inside her head, only never sung aloud. She placed the twig back inside her purse and closed the clasp. She gently rocked her handbag against her chest.

As the woman sat waiting for my response, I searched for some theory to process what she told me. I couldn't recall a thing, and I had no idea what to say. My eyes darted from one side of my brain like the lights at an active railroad crossing.

I hit a roadblock.

My therapy script was at a standstill.

We looked at each other for what seemed like a lifetime. "I think our hour is up," I said, lifting my wristwatch and leaning forward. "Let's pick this up next week." I opened the office door, and she passed by.

"Can I use your bathroom key?" she asked.

"Of course," I said, "Yes, of course. Please do."

She gripped the key in her palm as if entrusted with some honored relic. "Thank you so much," she said as if I had granted her a magical wish. Her eyes reached into mine. "Do you think anyone would mind if I walked around the halls? I want to walk around for a while. The floors have carpet, and the air is on. I miss being with people, and it's much cooler here."

"Wear a mask," I suggested, "I think it would be less concerning to everyone if you wore a mask. COVID things, you know." I paused. "You can leave your coat and purse and return for them."

She reached into her purse, took out her light blue surgical mask, and fitted it around her nose and mouth, leaving only the jumbled expressions in her eyes for me to know her mind. I noticed the twig she had shown me earlier clung to the side of her mask. Now faceless, she said, "I'm getting used to these things." The twig fell from the side of her mask to the floor by her foot. "I never liked bras either." She laughed.

After the woman left, I went to the restroom myself, exiting through the back door and turning corners. I noticed the woman walking in the hall, her heavy woolen coat hanging like a dusty Victorian drape, alone but hopeful, hugging her purse to her chest.

When I returned, the boy was sitting in the waiting room, and the twig was in the reception window. "I found that on the floor," he said, pointing with his rosy-red colored fingernail.

I reached for the twig and tossed it into the wastebasket. "Are you ready to come in for a chat?" I asked the boy.

I noticed yet another dusty moth in the window after we sat down. "Do you want me to kill it?" the boy asked, raising the rolled-up magazine.

"No, no, no," I said, scooping up the moth and putting it out. The powdery substance from its wings smudged my palm.

Many years ago, when I first went into private practice, I met a young man whose mother had recently died. I don't know if my memories are implicit or explicit, imagination or truth. Still, I remember parts of his story, separate pieces of a crazy quilt that I cannot guarantee will ever really fit together the way I reimagine it.

The boy told me his mother had been diagnosed with leukemia and died after a short, painless battle for life. He said, "My mother died," and stared blankly at me. I hesitated for a moment, imagining such an occurrence in my own life, and I said, "I'm sorry to hear that. How are you doing? Are you OK?" The boy grinned, then smiled and took a deep breath. "I knew this was a bad idea," he said. He motioned as if readying to leave.

"How so?" I asked, "Is it too soon for you?"

"Honestly," he said, "I don't care too much that she died. She was distant and didn't try to know or connect with me." He hung his head and quickly looked up. "I don't particularly like that you assume that I care. I wanted to talk with someone who didn't presume how I felt. My mother died, and I am not unhappy about it. Not even a little. I feel nothing." He sat for a moment. "Am I a bad person?" he finally asked. "I feel like what happened to her is karma. Still, shouldn't I feel something?"

Not knowing how to engage from the young man's perspective, I could only ask, "Did you have a chance to see her before she . . . left?"

"She didn't leave," he said, staring even harder at me, "She died," he quickly added, as if discussing the difference between an apple and a pear tree. "Her last words to me were that I was a disappointment, and that's the last thing she said to me."

"How, then, is her death a problem for you?" I managed to ask.

"It isn't," he said, staring back at me. "That's the problem. I wish my mother had given me something to mourn, and it's as if she were trying to take even that away from me."

"How can I help you with that?"

"I don't know."

As if fading from one scene to another, the boy with the fingernails raised his voice, "I'm not his bitch!" and brought me quickly back to the moment. "I've had enough of this," he said. He reached for a tissue and wiped softly under his eyes. "I'm moving out!"

At his age, which I assumed was in the late sapling stage, I imagined he could reshuffle the deck and rearrange his furniture. "What are you afraid of?" I asked.

"I'm afraid he is taking advantage of me."

"What would it mean if he took advantage of you?"

"I'd be a bitch!"

"Prove it."

"I can't prove it. I don't want to prove it."

"I'd recommend you prove it before that limb can grow sturdier."

"What are you talking about?'

"It's just this idea I have."

Emotional intelligence improvement suggests regularly thinking deeply and reflecting on our beliefs and actions. Without introspection, we can easily forget to live honestly with ourselves. The lived experiences we share with others, the *learning story*, can provide that purpose.

1. Mindfulness: paying attention to the present moment in a non-judgmental way.

2. Journaling: writing down thoughts and feelings to gain insight into oneself.

3. Self-inquiry: asking oneself questions to gain an understanding of one's thoughts, beliefs, and motivations.

4. Reflecting on past experiences: thinking about past events and how they have affected one's life.

5. Mediation: quieting the mind to gain a deeper understanding of oneself.

6. Therapy: working with a trained professional to gain insight into oneself and make positive changes.

7. Keeping a gratitude journal: recording things one is grateful for to focus on the positive aspects of one's life.

8. Setting aside time for introspection: regularly scheduling time to reflect on oneself.

A tree's life is in its roots, which control numerous vital processes by pumping nutrients across the whole plant, managing its overall health and balance. Apple trees often adjust to the harshest soil. The force of the winds forms sinewy or thicker limb structures and stronger or weaker connections with the earth. It seeks to establish complex root systems determined to reach a water source.

Like an apple tree, the human brain holds encoded information, ultimately enhancing or limiting its capacity to learn new information but not prohibiting it. Apple trees are encoded, like the human brain, to produce predictable results. Likewise, both can reach less-than-expected, incredible heights once established.

Fruit tree grafting allows for the growth of many fruits on a single rootstock. It takes practice and improved technique to succeed at this craft. When things turn out well, the grafting process allows the craftsman to reproduce favorite plants with consistent characteristics, enjoy early fruiting, and potentially have many types of fruit on one single tree.

Improved emotional intelligence is nearly exact to this model.

It takes work.

No one ever drowned in sweat.

9

The REBT In EI

The critical ingredient is getting off your butt and doing something. It's
as simple as that. A lot of people have ideas, but few decide to do
something about them now. —Nolan Bushnell

Psychological theory provides the EI practitioner with a model
for understanding thought, emotion, and behavior. EI draws from
existing, organized psychological ideas to establish its foundational
philosophy and related skills. EI theory depends on active, better-
informed emotional decision-making, using value-added skills for
whole-person well-being. EI theory proposes that those who engage its
principles will remain confident in their physical and emotional
wellness investment.

The main obstacles to emotional wellness, regardless of
practice orientation, are anticipatory and reminiscent thoughts.

Imaginative inner storytelling is the primary source of emotional disturbance and is not encouraged.

EI theory recognizes the interconnection between biology, psychology, and socio-environmental factors (biopsychosocial awareness). The essential components of EI include an improved understanding of these influences on well-being and how we operate collectively, physically, psychologically, and socially.

The foundation of emotional intelligence theory is biopsychosocial attentiveness. This model suggests that *people can never have only one disease.* There will always be an emotional connection when there is a physical illness. Likewise, we can expect a physical response when an emotional disturbance is present.

EI practitioners use a present, in-the-moment perspective for emotional data. Anticipatory thought (future-focused imaginative thinking) and retrospective thought (reminiscent of past stories) are the primary sources of depression and F^3 and the principal causes of emotional disturbance. EI practitioners do not emphasize the past or the future to resolve problems that we can more effectively address in the present moment. EI recognizes that the healthier option for the mind is in the present moment, where we can appreciate our choices and construct flexible, actionable plans.

EI practitioners know there is a difference between reliving and revisiting the past. For example, if we revisit the past for value-added information, we will likely build better-informed problem-solving skills. Likewise, we can make flexible plans. We cannot plan the future in any exact detail. We can only use our best judgment linked to some standard of probability.

We can change the plan without changing the goal.

Likewise, we can scrap the goal and create a new plan.

EI endorses the psychological ideas proposed in REBT and its ABC truth, science, and fact-based emotional problem-solving model.

REBT is a psychoeducational theory introduced by Albert Ellis, an American psychologist. He established his ideas in the 1950s, and REBT is a validated, meaningful approach to emotional problem-solving.

The ABC template makes REBT easy to use daily, helping to identify the irrational beliefs and maladaptive thoughts that can cause emotional and behavioral distress. REBT and its ABC paradigm help EI practitioners develop an informed skill for forcefully challenging maladaptive ideas and replacing them with more fact-based alternatives. REBT's ABC model can be shown as shorthand and appears as follows:

$$A + iB = C / D > E$$

Where **A** identifies the (**a**)ctivating event or the situation we are examining, the **iB** detects the irrational (**i**)(**b**)eliefs or thoughts we are using to describe the **A**. After pinpointing the Bs, the C isolates the emotional (**c**)onsequences or the emotional response. (The event is never the source of emotional upsetness. Our belief about the event causes the emotional consequences.)

Although not readily identified in the characteristic **ABC** model, are the **D** and the **E**, where the **D** provides a system of (**d**)isputation of the claims made at **iB**. Improvement in the **iB** results in an evolved **E** or the (**e**)motional (**e**)volution.

An alternative description of the **ABC** model may be:

- (**A**)ction: An Action is an observable event, situation, or circumstance. The Action is the particular event the practitioner wishes to explore more fully, e.g., "You said I was a bad mother, and that pissed me off!"

- **(iB)**elief: The beliefs used to interpret, perceive or think about the **A**. Beliefs represent our inner truth and create perception. We find our ideas, thoughts, and perceptions using the words *should, ought, must, have to,* and *need.* "This person should recognize that I am a perfect mother! This person should treat me well as a condition of my contentedness! I need them to cooperate with my expectations! I must be treated fairly by all people at all times. I need people to respect me, or I cannot be respectable! If someone mistreats me, it should not be that way. It must not be what it is! I cannot stand it."

- **(C)**onsequence: After relying on the beliefs at **iB** to establish your perception, we express an emotional consequence to it all: "I'm angry!" "I'm pissed!" I'm depressed." "I'm jealous." "I'm afraid!"

- **(D)**isputation: Disputation involves questioning the beliefs we use at **iB** that provoke emotional consequences. The simple question, "Is the belief I am using to understand this situation fact? Truth? Or is it my imagination?" can often suffice in getting things started. For example, *Is it true that I cannot be content when people judge me poorly? Is it true that I cannot stand it when people criticize me? Is it true that I need respect from everyone as a condition of happiness?* At the **D** or disputation, we circle back and account for our beliefs, seeking facts to replace fiction and imagination.

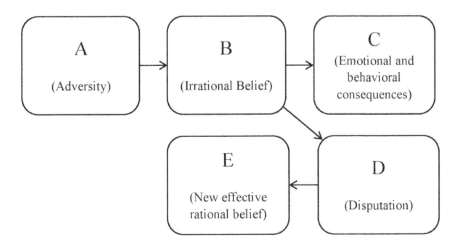

- **(E)**motional Evolution: Suppose we use truth, fact, and science to finetune our perception of the events, circumstances, and situations we encounter daily. We can express a more adaptive, less self-destructive emotional response to nearly any event, occasion, or condition.

REBT seeks to help consumers discover their irrational thinking tendencies, often characterized by demandingness, awfulizing, low frustration tolerance, and conditional self- and other-acceptance.

The **ABC** model explains the interaction between thoughts, emotions, and behaviors. Because teaching the model is a critical component of **REBT**, understanding this model of psychological problem-solving is an invaluable tool for improving emotional intelligence. REBT makes emotional intelligence improvement more operational.

As an EI therapist practitioner, I often meet people willing to engage in emotional problem-solving using the REBT strategy. I once met a man who hoped to improve his emotional intelligence by exploring his Fear of intimacy. The man was particularly concerned that he was unlovable and, therefore, not worthy or good enough for mature relationships. He had only one-night stands and short-lived romances that always ended severely to account for his attempts at romance. The man's destiny was for a lifetime of shallow, unfulfilling couplings. "I've never been in love," he said, hanging his head. "I don't know what is wrong with me."

He cried.

The man showed a magnitude of emotional range, shedding tears and quickly recovering with a smile as if prepared to conquer his goals with focus and enthusiasm, then suddenly diving deeply into despair. "I think I'm hopeless," he said. "My past haunts me. My parents couldn't get along. I don't know how to love because they didn't teach me. I had terrible teachers. How can I fix this?"

Overall, the man projected a robust, engaging personality that revealed underlying confidence and endurance in his 55 years. He showed significant resiliency in describing his professional background and adaptative skills for managing relationships with his employees. "I am a pretty good manager. I get along with the people who work for me. I think I'm a good leader. I can't have someone in my life for long—someone who cares about me and loves me. I seem to keep employees for years," he said when asked if he was committed to making his improvements. "It's time for me to settle down and do this thing. Everyone settles down. I don't know why I can't." He paused. "I think it's something to do with my mother. We had a terrible relationship, and she wasn't very agreeable."

"Maybe you're chasing a concept that isn't for you," I offered. "Where did you get the idea that what you do is not as good as your peers? Are your peers the standard for your choices?"

"My past is just not fulfilling. I need this."

"We try to avoid connecting with the past for what we are experiencing," I said. "We might ask ourselves, what does it mean that I can't mate with one person for the rest of my life?"

"I want to know *why* this isn't something I can have."

"EI improvement doesn't often seek to know *why*. Instead, we try to answer *how*," I said, setting the stage for coming. "We ask, 'How am I making myself feel the way I do?' 'What am I thinking at this moment?' 'How can I change the way I'm thinking now?' Nothing you can change about your past except how you think about it and reimagine it. Let's think about what you are telling yourself now about your past."

"I'm not used to thinking like that," he said, almost Fearfully. "This doesn't sound right to me. I thought what happened to me in the past makes me feel how I feel."

"Thoughts of the past can influence emotional expression. It isn't the past that forms our emotional response. It is our thoughts about the past that does that. If we leave thoughts unchallenged, we will repeat the same script and play the same character we've always played." I paused, looking for recognition. "Emotion comes from thinking and perception. We can reimagine the past and make ourselves anxious and depressed, and we can imagine the future and believe the past predicts the future. We can also consider the present moment and what we can do with it. What do you want to do with this moment?"

"I see."

"That was a real question."

"I want to get better."

"That's for the future. What about this moment?"

"I don't know what to do with only this moment."

"You could use it to accept yourself as you are without believing you can only be complete if you become someone else."

"That's a thought."

"The past is one resource for emotion. Reliving the past relies on selected memories, strengthened by believing that the past should not have happened." I paused. "That's what the word *why* will do for you every time. You will suddenly be thrust into the past, examining the *why* of the past rather than *how* to accept the past. We would be better off accepting our past. Acknowledgment of the past doesn't mean *liking* the past. You do not have to like what you accept. It is best to acknowledge what has happened without demanding that it hasn't happened."

"Yes, I do a lot of living in the past," the man said, suddenly aware. "Most of my thoughts are in the past, and I've moved in with it."

I pointed to the chair across from him. "You don't have to like that chair. You could wish it were a giraffe, but your wish won't change anything. You don't have to like your past, but you must accept it. Otherwise, you're choosing nuttiness over sanity. You can't do anything about anything that has ever happened. You can do everything about what you tell yourself about your past."

"There are a lot of chairs in my head I wish were giraffes." He hung his head. "I don't like living in the past."

"Move out!" I said, raising my voice ever so slightly. "You can expect to reminisce and revisit, but you've already handled everything. Good or bad, better or best, there isn't anything you can do to change it. You can think about it differently and accept it. No matter, you can't un-ring a bell."

The man gazed perplexedly. "I never heard anyone say that." He stared into his hands, "I always thought you had to make sense of the past to move on with your life."

"The past is imaginative, quilted squares of the most unpleasant events you can recall. We blind ourselves when we cover our minds with that quilt, and we lose what is possible in the present moment."

"I had some pretty bad experiences in my past," he said, anticipating that he may be able, at some point, to rid himself of his unpleasant memories. "I would like a way out." He refreshed his face with his hands, moving them over his eyes and down to his mouth, wiping away the tears. "I think it could have been better."

"Who knows, it could have been worse." I sipped from my paper Starbucks cup. "We only know what we know at the moment." I waited for a sign. "What you know now influences how you reimagine your past. We all could have done something better if we had known better. You can't change a single molecule of the past, but you can change how you think."

Returning to the **ABC** model, although there are several **As** (thoughts, events, or circumstances) in the man's story, we may start with the following:

(A) I have never had a long-term relationship.

The **A** is a space for identifying the event or thought the practitioner wishes to explore. It is often the most challenging part of explaining the model because it seems a more complicated step, but it isn't. The practitioner therapist asks, "What is on your mind?" and places that response beside **A**.

The **A** represents an event, a thought, or a circumstance, either from the past or the future, that the practitioner hopes to engage from a deeper perspective. The **A** should hold only the essential parts of the story. The **A**, as well, can change as the practitioner progresses through the **ABC** formula.

After establishing the **A**, the way was open to identifying the **iB**. "What are you afraid of when you tell yourself you have never had a long-term relationship?" I ask.

"Afraid?" he asks. "I'm not afraid of anything."

"When you think 'I am alone and will be alone forever,' what do you think that means about you?"

   (B) *"It means I need to be loved to be worthy of life. I'm unlovable, and I'm not good enough. It means I'm not a bad person!"*

"Ah!" I say, "You've found some **iBs**."

"I don't like **Bs**."

"They are workable **iBs**," I say, "I've heard these **iBs** before. You're not the only one. These **iBs** are buzzing around inside most people's heads, and even people who have long-term, intimate relationships feel the sting." I paused. "Your Bs are—everyone *should* love you; you *must* never make mistakes; you need a loving, long-term relationship to be content. Because you do not meet all of these conditions, you must be a terrible person!"

After identifying the **iB**, we begin searching for the **C** or the *emotional consequence* of having the **iB** and believing it is the indisputable truth.

It is common for people to believe that **A** causes **C**. The **ABC** paradigm exposes the **iBs** and improves the client's awareness that the **A** does not cause the **C**. The **iB** stings about the **A** are what drive the **C**.

> *(C)* *"Yes, that seems to sum it up pretty well. I'm pretty depressed and angry with myself."*

In search of the **D**, we may ask, "Prove to me *with evidence* that you are unworthy of intimate relationships. Prove to me with evidence that you are unlovable. Prove that you are not worthy of having one because you do not have a long-term relationship."

"I don't have any proof," he said. "I just know it."

> *(D)* *"Well, if there is no proof, you can undoubtedly unknow this self-defeating thinking. What is true about you and your skill at forming intimate relationships? What evidence can you use that is factual that you can use to defeat these cruddy ideas?*

"I think I'm worthy of a relationship with someone," he said, "I also think I *need* a relationship to *complete* me." The man paused for a moment, thinking. "Maybe I'm *desperate* for companionship to *prove* that I am worthy. I think I'm *desperate* because I'm afraid of what it means for me to be alone. I *need* someone in my life to make me feel better about myself." He looks directly at me. "I think I'm pretty selfish, and it's about me and how an intimate relationship can solve my problems. But it isn't about intimacy. It;'s about putting a bandaid over the real problem."

> *(E)* *Knowing these things about yourself, what can you do differently? How can you improve your thinking to*

produce a better, more self-improving idea of being alone?

"I could stop being so desperate and calm down my ideas. Get ahold of my illusions. I could learn to be content with myself as I am. I can't prove I'm no good or unworthy, but I believe it and always go with those ideas." He puts his head down and folds his arms over his knees. "If I believe something different, I will feel something different. If I did that, I wouldn't feel desperate and needy when I meet someone and start Fearing they will leave me."

"Good insight," I say. "Maybe if you were less needy and clingy, the person would want to stay longer."

"I think we're on to something."

"Yes," I say, "We found some new **As**."

REBT uses three main techniques, which correspond with the **ABCs**. Each learner might use a slightly different combination of methods depending on their past clinical experiences and individual symptoms (**iBs**).

- *Problem-solving techniques*

The ABCs can help us address the activating event (**A**). The techniques often improve alongside assertiveness, self-approving social skills, confident decision-making skills, and conflict-resolution skills.

- *Cognitive restructuring techniques*

These strategies help to change irrational beliefs (**iB**). They might include logical or rationalizing techniques, guided imagery and visualization, reframing or looking at events differently, humor and irony, and exposure to a Feared situation disputing irrational thoughts.

- *Coping techniques*

Coping techniques can help manage irrational thoughts and emotional consequences **(C)**. These coping techniques may include relaxation and meditation.

Regardless of the suggested techniques, we will likely have to put in some **ABC** work between sessions, allowing us to use and improve our skills in daily life. For example, you may use meditative techniques (mindfulness) with the **ABCs** when addressing situations we previously responded to aggressively or angrily. You may write your thoughts and perceptions before and after the experience.

Be aware that **REBT** is easy to practice badly, so practice is the key. Conveniently, the technique addresses secondary symptoms, such as becoming anxious about experiencing F^3 or feeling depressed about having depression—after an unsuccessful attempt at using the REBT method.

We cannot become discouraged if our efforts aren't paying off immediately. **The model offers insight. REBT and the ABCs are not the only techniques for improving emotional wellness**. After sufficient practice, we may be more self-improving, kinder, and more patient with others. EI encourages insight and confidence to seek an alternative if these are not the skills that suit your aspirations.

No one ever drowned in sweat

10

Our Stories of Ourselves

The stronger person is not making the most noise but the one who can quietly direct the conversation toward defining and solving problems.
—Aaron Beck

I have been reminded of a reviewer's comments of my book *Go Suck A Lemon: Strategies for Improving Your Emotional Intelligence*. The reader claimed to have never heard or read a functional definition of emotional intelligence. Nor had they heard of a compelling way to improve it. I completely understand. Everything about emotional intelligence improvement is easy to practice badly. EI is still a vague concept and could benefit from more research. It is much like its practitioners, who commit to a lifetime of introspection and self-acceptance.

Regardless of its seemingly unfinished composition, it's a good bet that advancing our understanding of emotion as a force in human life is a good idea, no matter how well we define it or how much work we put into the effort.

EI theory is an odd fellow, often referenced as emotional intelligence quotient (EQ); other times identified simply as emotional intelligence theory (EI). Our discussion presently is entirely related to emotional intelligence theory.

While some strongly associate emotional intelligence with a workforce leadership philosophy (EQ), others consider it a dynamic idea (EI) for improving overall emotional and physical health, emphasizing skill-building and application. Viewing emotional and physical fitness from a whole-person perspective, we challenge ourselves to be deliberative when making self-and-other assessments, drawing inferences, and addressing emotional challenges. Likewise, using the biopsychosocial (BPS) model, individuals can view themselves as multipart, whole persons, potentially better prepared to manage emotional and physical health through improved insight.

While numerous orientations in counseling today are determinist, the idea is that all events, including moral choices, are determined by experience. EI emphasizes that each moment can be unique and has few predictable outcomes. EI chooses evidence over expertise and takes a here-and-now, mindful perspective.

We tend to distort our worldview when we believe someone has mistreated us. We may assume, "I should be treated well under all circumstances, or I cannot stand it," or "I need to be loved to be worthwhile." These irrational thoughts reinforce our response, producing self-defeating and maladaptive behavior. If the thought cycle runs uninterrupted, it will invariably affect our physical and emotional health.

Managing reality distortions and stopping the mental spin requires insight-knowing what initiates the cycle, what perpetuates it, and what we can do to eliminate it. Once mindful of the triggers, people can learn to avoid awfulizing, catastrophic thinking.

Unpleasant thinking can alarm the mind and body, sending and receiving physical messages from our toes to our heads. The brain's limbic region signals that we are in danger, real or imagined. This siren numbs our ability to reason and produce rational thought. Chemicals fuel this alarm to the body responsible for F^3, limiting us to protective responses

A *bottom-up* approach to managing this response accepts that body sensation happens first, primarily using chemical messages. Managing stress hormones and managing the mind are both essential for overall well-being and can be interrelated. Stress can affect our physical and mental health. Moving from the toes to the head helps prioritize the body's response to Fearful thoughts, much like when a rowboat springs a leak. We begin with plugging the leak, not grabbing the oars and rowing to shore.

In the same way, when we are surging stress hormones into our bloodstream in response to something we Fear or would rather avoid. Our body springs a leak! We send glucagon, epinephrine (adrenaline), norepinephrine, cortisol, and growth hormones throughout our bodies. We must manage this deluge before using our brains for rational thinking.

Stress events or the leaks in our hull are frequently the results of emotional reflexes, memories, and automatic survival responses we've learned over a lifetime, causing the mind and body to feel unsafe and dysregulated. The bottom-up approach suggests an organized dual awareness for emotional management.

Begin by plugging the leak, and once the boat is seaworthy, our thoughts and the solutions we come up with for continuing the journey will be more likely to follow.

The part of the brain that develops earliest in life is the primitive brain, the brain stem. It is responsible for keeping us safe and where F^3 lays in wait. The primitive part of the brain does not suddenly turn off when the danger has passed. Repeated experiences can trigger thought and prompt the limbic system to store background information to respond predictably later on.

We might call this the Whack-A-Mole system.

We use our imagination to instigate ideas from our past and begin whacking them as they suddenly appear as potential hazards, derivatives of memory that we are sure will come up again and again. We may also call this the Imagine Dragons technique, where we slay one dragon only to imagine a hundred more coming at us over the horizon. Even those we've slain come back to life, only this time they have ten heads instead of one and bring all their friends and neighbors to feed on your Fears.

Once you understand *how* (never why) you think about something, you can change how you think about it. We cannot change our past image, but we can change how we think and behave when we reimagine our past. We can change what we tell ourselves about an event without addressing the underlying cause or the *why* that sends our limbic system into a never-ending spiral of thinking, never knowing.

We must seek alternatives to using only our heads to manage our self-defeating thoughts and emotions. We must look down at our toes and work through and deplete our stress hormones when we believe that hardship, ridicule, criticism, and failure are death sentences. We have to rid our bodies of the stress-producing substances that cement the physical prison in which we live.

When inconvenienced, bothered, or annoyed, we imagine ourselves in danger. EI suggests we are better off when we know the difference between real danger and imagined.

Our thoughts related to the past or the future often determine the intensity of our emotional arousal. Determinist philosophy endorses that past trauma, mainly childhood events, leads to abnormal behavior. By comparison, EI theory recognizes how reliving the past and predicting the future can cause F^3. It seeks to help individuals accept, not like, their history and avoid making detailed future predictions. We do not have to like what we accept, nor do we have to predict catastrophe to avoid it.

Acceptance recognizes that what has not happened cannot be predetermined, nor can the past be replayed. Thinking about a past or future event causes emotional expression, never imagined events. Our only connection to the past or the future is our thoughts about them, leaving only our views of these imaginative places the sole source for emotional intelligence improvement.

It's unlikely that our memory of anything is 100% accurate, leaving fragments, bits and pieces to represent what we recall. Instead, we rely on storytelling to identify our memories as reliably as the most recent story we told about an event. The slightest alteration to an account will become part of the story the next time we recall it, rendering the story and the storyteller incapable of distinguishing imagination from fact.

We seem forever to be asking ourselves *Why*.

From early childhood, nature has designed us to investigate even the most minuscule event. This phenomenon is often easy, and we do it without conscious awareness. Sometimes, however, an event from the past is left undefined and difficult to understand. So the mind attempts to process the memory until it finds a satisfactory answer, some conclusion that makes sense, and identifies the factors influencing our understanding of Why. We are often left with faulty, unstable memory to guide our search for meaning. Still, our mind will cycle a story persistently, seeking to understand the Why behind everything.

Retrospective thought can be harmful to an individual who nibbles daily. Our memories can become so ingrained that we have difficulty changing how we think about most things, particularly those we haven't fully understood. If we change some aspect of a story, that modification can spread like wildfire to answer other imagined questions about *why*. This persistent rumination increases emotional distress, which raises the risk of developing even more physical and emotional complications.

EI theory encourages practitioners to acknowledge that we cannot alter the past except by ruminating less or limiting ourselves. Because the past exists only inside our heads, understanding, uncovering meaning, and having unfinished business can lead to more altered versions and more unanswerable questions. Our recollections change, take on new dimensions, and evolve with time. Managing the past means putting an end to the endless, imaginative storytelling we use to answer the unanswerable, using our skill to create a self-improving inner dialogue to end it. There are familiar patterns of thinking common to those who relive their pasts and imagine their futures, occupying the mind with unnecessary stress and F[3]:

- *All-or-nothing thinking* often involves using absolute terms, such as never or ever. This faulty thinking can also include an inability to see the alternatives or solutions to a problem.

- When people *overgeneralize*, they conclude about one event and then incorrectly apply that conclusion across the board. For example, you get a bad grade on one math test and conclude that you're generally hopeless.

- *Catastrophizing* involves worst-case thinking and can be a prevalent cognitive distortion. Frequently, we Fear the uncertainty of potential adverse events, even despite a lack of objective facts to support their occurrence

- *Emotional reasoning* occurs when someone concludes that their emotional reaction to something defines its reality and engages in events from that perspective. Any empirical evidence is disregarded or dismissed in favor of the assumed truth of the feelings they are experiencing.

- *Should, Ought, Must, Have to, and Need statements* are covert demands, and we often use these words to validate irrational beliefs. We often feature these words in phrases like *You shouldn't dress like that!* or *You should always be polite! Or I need you to love me! Or I should succeed because I have to!*

- *Negative rumination* continuously focuses on the worst possible outcome, leading to inertia and feeling stuck, anxious, and depressed.

- **Overthinking** is when we dwell or worry about the same thought repeatedly. People can paralyze themselves using overthinking and struggle to make decisions or take action. Overthinking can be caused by and can contribute to depression, F^3, and other mental health disorders.

To adopt more rational thinking patterns, you must first become aware of your preferred ways of thinking. By cultivating mindfulness, you can acknowledge and identify the thinking patterns that have become habitual, then decide whether or not to engage them or change them. The skill of mindfulness creates a distance between yourself and your thoughts, allowing you to view yourself as separate from them:

- **Address Your Inner Critic**: Your inner critic loves convincing you of things that aren't true, often resulting in feelings of defeat and failure. Think of this voice as someone separate from you. Challenge the lies your inner voice tries to feed you. Ask yourself: Is that true? Is there evidence to back up that claim?

- **Recite a Mantra:** Reciting a mantra or rehearsed rational thought is a great way to pull yourself out from the irrational you create and into the present moment. You may use your mantra when your views counter your emotional goals. You can choose any word or phrase that will help bring you into the present and remind you to focus more on rational thinking. For example:

    o *I've handled this before and can process it better this time.*

- *Even this shall pass.*

- *I don't need your approval to be content in my life. I can be content all by myself.*

- *This challenge is familiar, and I can manage it.*

- *I am safe.*

- *I am enough without approval.*

- *I am complete as I am.*

- *I do not need anything.*

- *Nam-myoho-renge-kyo.*

- ***Change Your Surroundings***: Sometimes, your thoughts can seem so loud that you can change your physical surroundings. Take a walk in Nature, run, or meet up with a friend. Engage in a self-improving cycle to return to the problem with a clearer headspace. Choose an activity or location that you find enjoyable and feel better. If you need the company of others, surround yourself with people who will encourage your positive thinking.

Self-destructive thinking patterns can be hard to break, particularly when habitual. You cannot quickly untangle thinking patterns strengthened by years of repetition. You must instead be compassionate and patient with yourself as you work toward your emotional goals.

A person's ability to change perspectives when faced with an unfortunate event or occurrence is an essential measure of success in improved EI. Attitude is all about choices; how you frame your mind around a situation determines how you will feel about it.

Perspective is like attitude or mindset. You will express distortion and misassemble truth if you have a distorted view. For example, if you believe you are not being appreciated and think you need to be appreciated by others as a condition of living contentedly, you have used a self-damaging mindset to address a situation that holds only the meaning you give it. You may say, *Being appreciated is nice. At this moment, being valued is important to me. My boss is not praising me, and I am unhappy. I can't make my boss praise me. But I can change my perspective. I can accept this situation for what it is, not what it should, must, or has to be. I don't need my boss's approval to be content. I'd like it, but I certainly don't need it.*

Emotional intelligence emphasizes that truth, fact, and science are the best sources of emotional information in all situations, particularly those we find uncomfortable or disturbing. Seeking truth through science and fact is likely to provide a balanced perspective. For example, the dialogue above makes it more accurate than not being praised can be endured and not an expected catastrophe. It is more accurate that being honored is not an essential component of contented living. If we believe we cannot endure life without praise, we are anxious, outraged, and possibly depressed when we don't get it. Of course, being ignored isn't pleasant when we engage in a task and help achieve an outcome. But it is endurable and not a necessity of life to be valued. Likewise, if we demand praise, we are not likely to believe it is authentic, leaving us unsatisfied.

One confounding factor in managing F^3 using perspective-changing is that our minds are not often in the situation we're addressing. We are often distracted by our imagination of how the problem will interfere with our lives in the future. Faced with discomfort, disturbance, and disorder, we tend to lose sight of the situation because we imagine what the condition will cause to happen next-somewhere in time. Essentially, much of the effort we put into resolving a problem gets overrun with dragons and monsters from our imagination of how it will impact us later.

The future- and past-focused mind is default for human reason. This habit of forecasting the future doesn't just arise in everyday occurrences. Future thinking is like a virus in our review about most things, as if telling a story and beginning at the end. Our inner story is rarely about what is happening but what we believe could happen. Our default mental state is to lean forward, off the axis of time, often making dismal predictions of what to expect.

Researchers suggest that we spend around 47 % of our day imagining our future. When we're not doing that, we're reimagining our past or combining the two. Consequently, the more we engage in life from these perspectives, the more we feel unhappier and anxious.

Emotional intelligence practitioners are encouraged to interrupt the natural potential; we all must imagine the future and the past with curiosity while choosing to address the present moment and manage the challenges we are genuinely facing. In other words, we don't need to change what we are doing but how we are doing it. Rather than running blindly into the darkness, we can be more interested and less afraid.

For many of us, it's difficult, if not impossible, to escape the first thought we have about the circumstances of life. Our first thought will likely be the perspective we take about anything. The human brain can only think of one thing at a time and usually won't let go of the first thought until it finds answers. The belief is that everything will fall apart and life as we know it will end unless we somehow prevent it. Those are imaginations of the future and what could happen if we engage our stress response and disable rational thinking. To attempt to break away from the first thought takes time and practice.

Improved emotional intelligence encourages the second thought you can have in any situation you face if you can summon it. Thinking strategies along these lines are essential to addressing the intensity and duration of our self-destructive use of past and future thinking.

Stoic philosopher Epictetus once admonished that *people are not disturbed by things but by their perception of things.* Put differently, we're not anxious because of the obstacles we face, only our thoughts about them. This approach to emotional problem-solving doesn't involve changing the outer circumstances. Instead, it encourages us to perceive obstacles differently and examine the real challenges. That effort requires thinking about thinking or thinking more than once.

People cannot multitask.

It is a myth.

The human brain cannot perform two tasks requiring high-level brain function simultaneously. Most surprisingly, studies show that we aren't multitasking when we think we're multitasking. We shift rapidly between tasks. We can only think of one thing at a time, but we can alter our thoughts, providing us the key to managing F^3 through mindful awareness.

Our brains are hardwired to collectively manage specific, day-to-day activities, making those thoughts almost imperceivable. Regardless, they are individual thoughts with apparent answers that the brain puts little attention into managing; it can instantaneously process them with little or no effort.

Neurological science has demonstrated that the human brain does not respond so quickly when it believes it is in real danger or perceives a threat. It's as if everything slows down, and the spotlight is only on the threat; the nucleus of existence becomes our central focus. We become fixated on what could, might, will, or won't happen, and we start problem-solving, primarily using our imagination of the future.

We think, *what if this* and then *what if that*?

We use *what-if* statements to check the possible pain threshold or the imagined difficulty of the potential obstacle. *If* the condition is confirmed, we run a block of statements (called the *if-block*); we process another block of statements (called the *else-block*). Suddenly our attention has narrowed, consumed with a single thought that jumps from one imaginary outcome to another.

I am not immune from this thought cycle, but I have successfully learned to think a second time, changing the direction of my thinking to something more fact-, science-, and truth-based.

Later in this book, we will discuss managing the internal terror we often create with our imagination. For now, we can engage with our thoughts curiously. Start with the small stuff, traffic jams, failing at anything, and criticism. Make some effort, even the smallest, to observe your mind and entice it to do something else-just a nudge. You might imagine a field of cows in place of monsters on the horizon.

- *Create a cue*: One of the critical insights we can achieve using emotional intelligence is increasing self-awareness through more adaptive habit formation. Let's imagine a field of cows.

- Breathe deeply.

- Hear the sounds.

- Fill your lungs with clean air and exhale, visualizing your breath as it escapes the warmth of your body into the chilly air.

- Feel the sensation of the rain on your skin. Taste it.

- Picture the insects buzzing around the cow pies.

- Breathe them in.

- You might say, *Everything is better with some cows around* and smile broadly.

- Nod your head in approval.

- Breathe deeply, smile and as you exhale, nod your head in approval and acceptance.

Most people who make plans to change their thinking will often not plan for inaction or failure. We don't always remember, or we find it challenging to engage in our emotional management plan as it unfolds, and we are likely to go with our first thought rather than the second. It may feel counterintuitive in distress to manage the mind and body instead of the monsters you imagine.

When something feels *counterintuitive*, it goes against what we believe would be logical or against common sense. For example, if your intimate mate decides he's leaving you after thirty years of marriage, it would be counterintuitive to breathe deeply, smile, and nod your head. It may take weeks, months, or even years to engage in this activity, but when you manage to do it, do it! A counterintuitive proposition is not likely to be true when assessed using the information available. Our action plans can be quickly dismissed and become inaction.

Sometimes, you will either not remember your action plan or fall back into what you have always done. When this happens (and most certainly will), remind yourself of your plan and carry it out! At this beginning stage of your EI improvement, it is crucial to create new, habit-forming behaviors, even when you forget to use them. Your skill-building habits do not have to be in real-time.

Plan early for imperfection.

These changes in perception and meaning involve actions rather than inactions, skill-building against habituated responses, and a present rather than future-focused, resulting in controllable rather than uncontrollable emotional engagement.

No one ever drowned in sweat.

11

Hormotional

The best years of your life are when you decide your problems are your own. You do not blame your mother, the ecology, or the president; you realize that you control your destiny. —*Albert Ellis*

The mind and body will integrate, adapt, and learn to survive wherever an infant is born. Nature's coordination between known and unknown is the foundation for all adaptive behavior.

We are ready-made for life anywhere, preset to learn social behavior and adapt to change. Nature only allows for the transmission of scrambled DNA to improve our chances of survival and procreation. Our principal nature is to live in groups, collaborate, and cooperate. Only when exposed to others' ideas, can we discern right from wrong, good from evil, and better from worse. If the world were to crumble and we survived, our first impulse would be to find other survivors. Our collaborating and cooperating skills would become much more pronounced than now. Being accepted and needed would be a daily obligation. Our ideas of the good, bad, better, best, friend, foe, right, and wrong would also undergo some adjustment.

Researchers have described the human brain as a *tableau rasa* or blank slate at birth, Nature's attempt to make adaptation more possible. Of course, the human brain is never empty. You may imagine a blackboard instead. Erased, chalky residue, barely visible, words and symbols written over, identifiable marks, messages left to us by our ancestors lodged in our DNA.

Depending on our paternities, it is likely that our brains contain latent or lingering particles of DNA that replicate, during gestation, in some distinctive combination. Nature's logic may be that the traits found in each of us were probably responsible for thousands of years of successful co-living and procreation. The likelihood that these genetic traits will result in increasingly more viable offspring if we replicate our DNA is the probable master plan.

In that same regard, Nature sets out to make it possible for these DNA elements to arrange themselves in different ways, offering a chance that an offspring will assimilate into and be progressively more helpful to future generations.

Just as blood type, hair color, eye color, and facial features are congenital, personality is likely predetermined. While we might describe Nature's impact on our development as pre-wiring, chiefly influenced by genetic inheritance and other biological factors, nurture has been considered the vital influence of the environment on personality. Maternal stress, F[3], and depression, along with other pressures on prenatal development, can and likely prevail upon a maturing embryo, and fetus exposure to the stress hormones produced by the mother when in distress can influence prenatal psychological development and may impact behavior in later life.

Nature emphasizes revision and modification over the strength of inherited traits, so humans adapt, making emotional improvement a component of human survival. Personality, however, cannot be modified—only the behaviors we develop along with our genetic temperament. A battle with genetics over learned behavior is often the most significant conquest.

Both Nature and Nurture influence human development. Each of these components can affect the other to the extent that there is always a delicate balance between them, allowing for a variation to accommodate success, failure, growth, and change. For example, if Nature has dictated that an individual's personality may include a tendency for resilience, that person may thrive under the most adverse circumstances. On the other hand, if an individual does not possess an inherited potential for this type of strength, that person may develop this characteristic through repeated and focused experience. Likewise, individuals predisposed to flexibility may engage in the same challenge with similar results.

Relying on resilience and flexibility may make these demanding behavioral modifications. If not already part of the individual's predetermined psychological personality, assembling these traits would be possible, but the primary consideration is to overcome learned behavior.

Nature cooperates with Nurture by helping sustain life, endure hardship, and establish balance. The resourceful limbic system, located within the brain, is the mechanism of this delicate partnership. The limbic system allows for rest, relaxation, and quickly resuming everyday living to be alerted and routed for self-protection and well-being.

We are at our best in homeostatic balance when eating, sleeping, and engaging in social activities. If something threatens us, we respond quickly, purposefully, and without much thinking. We return to homeostatic balance when we believe we are safe.

The limbic system is a set of structures in the brain that controls emotion, memories, and arousal. It contains regions that detect Fear, bodily control functions, and sensory information. All the limbic system components work together to regulate some of the brain's most important processes.

The limbic system is critical to how much motivation we express in achieving goals and when and under what circumstances we direct emotion and its related behaviors. Our design utilizes the Fear response and extinguishes it when no longer required.

You may imagine hunting in the jungles of Las Vegas 10,000 years ago. You stop by the water's edge, examine a seashell, and listen to a volcano rumbling somewhere in the distance. You sense something approaching and look up, only to see a wolf coming toward you. Before you know it, you find yourself in a tree, panting.

The wolf passes beneath the tree, looks up at you, pees on the tree, and wanders into the thick brush. After taking a deep breath and releasing it, your communication pathway to the limbic system signals safety. You climb down from the tree and resume your food search.

In response to acute (F^3) stress, we activate the body's sympathetic nervous system after the sudden and involuntary release of stress hormones. The primary hormones affected are:

Cortisol: The body manufactures this stress hormone in response to actual or imagined emergencies helping cope with problems quickly. In balance (non-stress), the body's cells use 90% of its energy in metabolic activities such as repair, renewal, or formation of new tissues. When stressed (F^3), our brain sends messages to the adrenal glands to release more cortisol. Likewise, this hormone signals the release of glucose into the blood to provide more significant amounts of energy to the muscles. This automatic response does not affect our body once the hormonal levels are normal. If we are under stress regularly, cortisol levels continuously increase, burning unnecessarily, and freezing the functions of recovery, renewal, and creation of new tissues leading to hormonal deregulation and potential disease.

Glucagon: This hormone acts on the metabolism of carbohydrates and synthesizes them in the pancreas. The primary function of glucagon is to allow the liver to release glucose stored when our body has low levels of this substance and needs a more significant amount to function correctly. The role of glucagon is to be the opposite of insulin. Insulin decreases high glucose levels; glucagon increases them when too low. When we have F^3, our pancreas releases considerable amounts of glucagon to provide more energy to our body; deregulating our hormonal functioning is especially dangerous for those with diabetes.

Prolactin: The anterior pituitary gland secretes this hormone and is responsible for stimulating the milk secretion of women during lactation. When a woman is lactating, she can produce milk by releasing this hormone. High F^3 can cause hyperprolactinemia— increased prolactin which inhibits the hypothalamic hormone. Rising prolactin levels, the hormone that synthesizes female sex hormones, are inhibited, causing a lack of ovulation, estrogen decrease, and a lack of menstruation.

Estrogens: F^3 reduces the synthesis of estrogens, which can alter the sexual functioning of women. The relationship between estrogen and stress is bidirectional; F^3 can facilitate the creation of estrogens, but in turn, estrogens may constitute a hormone that protects against stress.

Progesterone: This hormone produced in the ovaries regulates women's menstrual cycle. Experiencing F^3 for long periods can decrease the production of this hormone, creating a progesterone imbalance that can lead to various symptoms such as decreased sex drive, excessive tiredness, weight gain, headache, or mood changes.

Testosterone: This hormone promotes the male sex drive and allows for the growth of reproductive tissue. It also enables the development of secondary sexual characteristics such as facial and body hair or sexual erections. When a male is in F^3 regularly, testosterone levels decrease as the body chooses to use its energy to produce other hormones, such as cortisol. In this way, F^3 becomes one of the leading causes of sexual problems such as impotence, erectile dysfunction, or lack of sexual desire. Lowering levels of this hormone can produce mood swings, constant fatigue, and an inability to sleep and rest properly.

Adrenaline: Produced by the adrenal glands after receiving a message from the brain that a stressful situation has presented itself, adrenaline causes that overwhelming immersion of the body into a state of F^3. Along with norepinephrine, adrenaline is mainly responsible for our immediate reactions when we are afraid. Your muscles tense; your breathing is faster; you may sweat. Along with the increase in heart rate, adrenaline also provides a surge of energy, allowing you to run and narrow your focus on escaping.

Norepinephrine: Like adrenaline, norepinephrine is an arousal hormone. Norepinephrine makes you more aware, awake, focused, and responsive to threats. It also helps shift blood flow away from areas where it might not be so crucial, like the skin, and toward more essential areas, like the muscles, to flee the stressful scene. Although norepinephrine might seem redundant, given adrenaline (also called epinephrine), we have both hormones as a backup system. If the adrenal glands are not working well, you still want something to save you from catastrophe. Depending on the long-term impact of the stress and how you handle it could take anywhere from half an hour to a couple of days to return to a normal resting state.

The link between F^3 and hormonal functioning is clear. Constant or regular pressure without a factual source for its activation can lead to severe psychological and physiological consequences. Stress can lead to severe health issues when the body continuously and chronically releases cortisol. Too much cortisol can suppress the immune system, increase blood pressure and sugar, decrease libido, produce acne, contribute to obesity, etc. Although estrogen and testosterone also affect how we react to stress.

Improvement in emotional intelligence involves gathering biological, psychological, and social resources to recognize how we engage with real and imagined threats. When we face real danger, such as a lion, a bear, or a skunk, we will employ the F^3 response for its intended purpose. When someone cuts in line, when we take a test, wait for bad news, or disagree, our bodies hear the same alarm and activate the F^3, our resistance to perceived harm.

Where, in the wild, we may never encounter an unfriendly, uncooperative, and insulant customer service person, we will, without much thought, use our senses (sight, sound, smell, hearing) to draw rapid conclusions from memory, concurrently initiating the same hormonal response we used to defeat the wolf or swat a dodgy insect.

The prefrontal cortex links to the limbic system and is the part of the brain that controls emotional expression, problem-solving, memory, language, judgment, and sexual behaviors. Nature designed these circuits to respond to a real and imaginary threat simply by their proximity to structures in the limbic system, such as the amygdala, the thalamus, and the hippocampus.

EI theory is a complex interaction between human biology, philosophy, and social modeling, constant, dynamic communication between the mind and the body, ultimately producing our unique emotional ecology. Our biggest hurdle in improved emotional intelligence is to use the rational part of the cortex to take control of the irrational emotions of the limbic system. After learning about this brain system and its related anatomy, EI encourages building skills to change how your limbic system responds to an imagined threat.

It can take some work.

No one ever drowned in sweat.

12

The Nature of Nurture

There is in everyone at every stage a new miracle of vigorous unfolding. —Erik Erikson

EI includes in its theoretical construct the influence of psychosocial development. Psychosocial development is a theory in psychology that refers to the expression of an individual's personality and how social experiences shape it throughout their life. The idea was proposed by Erik Erikson, who believed that an individual's personality develops through a series of stages, each of which is characterized by a specific psychosocial crisis that needs to be resolved. These stages include trust vs. mistrust, autonomy vs. shame and doubt, initiative vs. guilt, industry vs. inferiority, identity vs. role confusion, and intimacy vs. isolation. Each stage builds upon the one before it and is essential for developing a healthy personality.

Human development is summarized simply as a skill and deficit-building process, a progression through life that is always engaged and influenced by our prior encounters. Establishing the elemental concept of trust as the ground floor of our initial and ongoing human journey may be Nature's commentary on encountering others later on in life. If achieved, we can expect the basic concept of trust to withstand the weight of the seven additional layers of experience we will likely place upon it.

Infancy, early childhood, middle childhood, adolescence, early adulthood, middle adulthood, and old age are the age-specific periods of human life. These stages may represent a coordinated pattern of psychosocial expression, culminating in the particular strengths and deficits to meet the predictable crises inherent in addressing living humans' challenges. We propose eight stages of human psychosocial development, but we should remember that this is a theory for understanding human psychosocial development. We may not grow definitively, but we seem to grow with predictability. We may sometimes develop in one dimension and not in another unevenly. We may grow partially. We may be mature in one realm and childish in another. The past, present, and future mingle and pull us backward, forward, or toward the future. We are, nevertheless, made up of layers and constellations of cells.

First Phase of Human Psychosocial Development / Stages 1-4

- o   **Seed Germination**

- o   **Rooting & Budding**

- o   **The Discovery of the I**

1.   **Trust / Mistrust** is the first stage of human psychosocial development. This stage begins at birth and continues until approximately 18 months of age. During this stage, infants are uncertain about their world and look toward their primary caregiver for stability and consistency of care. If care is consistent, predictable, and reliable, the infant will develop a sense of trust that they will carry into future relationships.

Conversely, mistrust, suspicion, and F^3 may develop in the developing infant if we do not consistently provide these words. From that perspective, the infant may not have enough confidence in the people around them or their ability to influence others to provide help or comfort. Infants who achieve trust in this stage are more capable of handling social threats and are more hopeful.

Failing to acquire trust may lead to the development of social Fear. Infants who develop a sense of mistrust will carry it into other relationships. Infants who do not achieve confidence will likely express higher than usual F^3 levels and heightened insecurity.

The key to the theory is that an infant who develops mistrust during this period will likely engage in the next developmental stage with a deficit. We can expect an infant with a balanced view of trust to encounter the next developmental stage with a more adaptive outlook.

2.   **Autonomy / Shame and Doubt** is the second stage, following the stage of Trust / Mistrust, which occurs between 18 months to approximately three years of age. Children develop a sense of personal control over physical skills and independence.

Success in this stage leads to willpower, self-discipline, and determination. If children in this stage are encouraged and supported in their increased independence, they become more confident and secure to engage confidently.

Children who are encouraged to be more independently mobile discover individual competencies. A willingness to engage in dressing, grooming, choice-making, and self-control begins to appear at this age and should be encouraged and lead to the child's growing sense of independence and autonomy.

If children are criticized, overly controlled, or not allowed to assert themselves, they may feel inadequate and unable to endure hardship. Instead, they may over-depend on others, lack self-acceptance, and express shame or doubt in their emerging skills and deficits. As an example of the continuum of psychosocial development, a child who manages to develop trust is more likely to build autonomy in the next life period. A child who bears the deficit of mistrust will not likely engage in independence and express neediness and dependency later in life.

3.   **Initiative / Guilt** is the third stage of human psychosocial development, beginning at three years and lasting until five. Children start to assert themselves more frequently at this age. Although the

caregiver may perceive aggression, children are better encountered with patience to provide a continuum of normal child development.

Playing is central to this stage of life, as it allows children to explore their interpersonal skills through initiating activities. Children plan activities, make up games, and stir events with others.

We expect children to develop a sense of initiative and feel secure in leading others and making decisions. Conversely, suppose we inhibit initiative through criticism or control or the lingering residual of low mistrust, shame, and doubt. In that case, children can develop a sense of guilt and impair initiative development. The outcome may be that the child will overstep his forcefulness with others, causing the parent to punish the child who restricts the initiative's expression too much.

It is at this stage, as well, that the child will begin to ask many questions as the desire for knowledge begins to grow. Suppose the caregiver treats the child's questions as trivial, a nuisance, embarrassing, or threatening. In that case, the child may feel guilty for being a nuisance and Fear learning because it can lead to criticism and ridicule. Too much guilt can cause a child to interact with others and inhibit their creativity slowly. Of course, some accountability is necessary; otherwise, the child would not know how to exercise self-control, and restraint and be motivated by conscience.

4.   **Industry (competence) / Inferiority (incompetence)** occurs between five and twelve. Children are at the stage where they will likely be learning to read and write, do mathematics, and be more independent. Teachers begin to take on an essential role in the child's life as they teach the child-specific skills requiring rote memory and reward for achievement.

At this stage, the child's peer group will gain greater significance and become a significant source of the child's sense of self. When we provide the child with ample opportunity to win approval by demonstrating specific societal competencies, it will likely achieve competence. The child often begins to express a sense of pride in their accomplishments. Children begin to feel industrious (competent) and more confident in achieving goals; if they are encouraged and reinforced to demonstrate initiative, they expect to feel industrious (capable). If the initiative is not enabled, if parents or teachers restrict it, the child may feel inferior, doubt their abilities, and not reach their potential. Suppose we do not allow the child to develop a specific skill. If they see their friends and neighbors achieving, they may feel inferior. However, failure is necessary for normal child development because it can lead to modesty.

Phase Two of Human Psychosocial Development / Stage 5

- **Root Spread**
- **Leafy Development**
- **Fruit Formation**
- **The Birth of a sense of I**

5.   **Identity / Role Confusion** is the fifth stage of development and begins to emerge at 12, lasting until 18 years. Adolescents search for a sense of self during this stage by exploring personal values, beliefs, and goals. During adolescence, the transition from childhood to adulthood is most important. Children are becoming more independent and looking at careers, relationships, families, and housing.

Children in this development period express a deeper connection to society and the desire to fit in while maintaining a sense of individuality. In the moratorium, the adolescent mind is the stage between childhood and adulthood, between the child's morality and ethics.

Identity development is a fundamental challenge contributing to overall adult psychosocial performance, a significant stage where the evolved identity will occupy adulthood. The adolescent will re-examine previous developmental milestones (from birth to present) and form an adult identity during this stage.

This development period engages two opposing selves: the Sexual and the Occupational. Ultimately, this stage should culminate in an integrated sense of self, what one wants to do and be, and an appropriate sex role. Success in this stage will lead to fidelity or the ability to commit to others based on acceptance, even with ideological differences. Failure to establish a sense of identity within oneself and society can lead to role confusion. Role confusion can be observed in individuals not being sure about themselves as emerging adults or their place in society.

Third Phase of Human Psychosocial Development / Stage 6

- **Full Foliage**

- **Pollination**

- **Reproduction**

- **The Expression of I**

- **The Birth of a sense of We**

6.   **Intimacy / Isolation** is the sixth stage involving young adults between 18 and 40. This stage's primary conflict is forming intimate, loving relationships with another person. We begin to share ourselves more intimately, exploring relationships that lead to long-term commitments. Completing this stage can result in intimate relationships and a sense of responsibility, safety, and care. Avoiding intimacy and Fearing commitment and relationships can lead to isolation, loneliness, and depression. Success in this stage will lead to the virtue of love.

Fourth Phase of Human Psychosocial Development / Stage 7

- **Fruit Harvest**

- **Seed Spreading**

- **The Expression of We**

- **The Search for Me**

7.   *Generativity / Stagnation* is the seventh stage. This stage takes place during middle adulthood (ages 40 to 65). Generativity refers to making a mark on the world through creating or nurturing things that will outlast the individual. People experience a need to develop or promote something that will survive them, often hoping to make a positive change that will benefit others. We achieve generativity by raising children, being productive at work, and participating in community activities and organizations. We develop a sense of being a part of the bigger picture through generativity. Success at this stage leads to feelings of usefulness and accomplishment. At the same time, failure may result in shallow involvement in the world by failing to find a way to contribute, living stagnant, and being unproductive.

Fifth Phase of Human Psychosocial Development / Stage 8

- o **Ripe Harvest**

- o **Seed Hardening**

- o **Dormancy**

- o **The Merging of I, We, and Me**

- o **A Sense of Us**

8.   *Ego Integrity / Despair* is the eighth and final stage of psychosocial development. This stage begins at approximately age 65 and ends at death. During this time, we contemplate our accomplishments. We seek to develop an acceptance of ourselves and others and balance our view of our successes and failures.

Integrity is a process of esteeming our lives using self-and-other acceptance and patience. Integrity at this stage represents acceptance of our lives and those we have met. It is a period of building cohesion and wholeness. Conversely, suppose we view our lives as unproductive. In that case, if we feel guilty about our past, believe we have been poorly treated, think we have mistreated others, suppose we did not accomplish our life goals, and cannot accept, tolerate or be patient with our memories, we can expect to become dissatisfied with life and develop a sense of despair.

Despair often leads to depression, hopelessness, and enduring dread and desperation. Success in this stage will lead to the virtue of wisdom. Wisdom enables a person to look back on life with closure and completeness, accepting death's inevitability without Fear. We do not characterize wise people as having a continuous state of ego integrity, but instead by integrating themselves with others equally.

We can describe the human brain as an apple tree in a full canopy. Complete with a trunk, a root system, and branches bearing fruit, its design reflects the promise of life in plants and animals, enabling adaptation, accommodation, resiliency, and endurance.

At birth, the average human brain is about a quarter of the size of the average adult brain, doubling in size in the first year of life, adding an estimated 250,000 neurons every minute. The human brain grows after birth and is about 80% of its potential adult size by two.

As an infant matures, the connections between these cells make the brain work uniquely. The networks between brain cells and later cell clusters become the links between brain function and experience. Ready or not, we construct an operational adult brain that endeavors to adjust, adapt, and endure.

Although early childhood is critical in brain development, particularly the parts essential for language acquisition, selecting active over inactive neural circuits is a lifelong process, always ready for adaptive change, pliable, elastic, and flexible plastic.

The human brain has the unique ability to reorganize itself by forming new connections between brain cells. Brain plasticity or neuroplasticity is the brain's ability to modify its connections or rewire itself. As we age, the brain-change rate declines but does not stop. On the contrary, we now know that new neurons can appear in certain brain parts until we die. The brain's plasticity, particularly the human brain, plays a central role in the normal development of neural systems, allowing for adaptation and response to both exogenous and endogenous input. The responsibility of those who seek EI improvement is to know the brain's potential for reshaping and using it.

EI improvement can take some be work.

No one ever drowned in sweat.

13

Comparison Shopping

Rational discussion is worthwhile only when a significant base of shared assumptions is substantial. —Noam Chomsky

EI may be nothing more than a paradox inherent in each of us but left undefined without curiosity to fuel it. It may be a product of self-assessment, a framework for managing emotional behavior, navigating social complexities, and making better decisions leading to better outcomes. In an article entitled *Emotional Intelligence* in the journal *Imagination, Cognition, and Personality* in 1990, authors Peter Salovey and John Mayer proposed the idea of emotional intelligence, but only as a curiosity-a potential for building a more solid, data-driven theory, possibly by someone else more interested in doing that.

Daniel Goleman later popularized emotional intelligence (EQ) in his 1996 book *Emotional Intelligence*. Despite the measurement obstacles for gauging EI, the evidence in favor of scientifically identifying what constitutes emotional intelligence is accumulating. The current theoretical framework, however, has led only to establishing it as an idea worth exploring.

As we dovetail the identified factors common to EI/EQ, we may suggest that the theory offers skills for pinpointing and managing one's emotions (self-awareness) and being more emotionally with others (other-awareness). We may propose three principal skills common to both theories:

- The ability to be emotionally attentive or competence to identify and name emotions in ourselves and others;
- The ability to utilize our emotional awareness and apply it to thought management and problem-solving, and
- The ability to manage emotion, including regulating one's thoughts and feelings.

There is a budding industry growing around the idea of EI. Tests and evaluations (often at a cost) propose an emotional intelligence quotient (EQ) that can be concretely and scientifically determined. As of this writing, no validated psychometric test or scale for gauging or identifying emotional intelligence exists, making EI more a concept, a notion, and unscientific. Paying customers beg to know their EQ, so someone satisfies that desire. Emotional intelligence may have a direct relationship to social norms. Because these norms are constantly in flux, so is EI, rendering it more likely a curiosity and not subject to rigid scientific explanation.

For example, is your current manner of managing emotional expression working for you? The answer to that question is too individualized, dependent on experience, and wholly related to subjective adaptability. We couldn't endorse that calm, measured, rational thinking is likely the best way to adapt to a warzone or live with tarantulas. Applying science to EI would be much like conjuring data to support the benefits of Catholicism over Judaism, belly dancing over waltzing, and Democrats over Republicans.

EI is an adaptive *lifestyle* or a system of operational beliefs that help manage our emotional life from a flexible social construct. Is your emotional dynamic supple, elastic, and plastic? Or is it rigid, stiff, and immovable?

You decide.

There you will discover your budding for correction.

The critical factors in identifying and quantifying EI depend on self-awareness and honest self-assessment. This process does not mean excluding the opinions of others. A suitable combination of factors, weighted more on self-understanding, is probably the best gauge of EI. For instance, we may assess our emotional range as well-adjusted, balanced, and neither extreme nor muted. By contrast, those we engage with regularly may have a different assessment of us. We may believe our anger, jealousy, or guilt concerns us and others and could use a more profound examination. It's hard to say. A problem with closed-minded people is their mouth is always open. You are the final judge of your self-appraisal. We can begin our self-assessment by identifying some personality traits and related behaviors thought to be the promises of improved EI:

Robust Emotional Vocabulary

EI improvement finds strength in the use of vocabulary and language. While people might describe themselves as simply feeling bad, people who practice EI can pinpoint the inner language (the thinking) used to conceptualize the outward expression of emotion and the word we use to describe it. The more specific the word choice that describes our state of mind, the more insight we can achieve. Insight into spoken and internal language can lead to better awareness.

Curiosity

Rather than seeking a result from improved EI, interest and curiosity in the process will likely lead to better self-awareness. Curiosity may stand as one of the more critical indicators of the EI practitioner. Developing a curious awareness of the mind, asking, *Where is my mind? Do I imagine the future? Reimagine the past. What conclusions am I drawing? How am I making my mind work this way?* requires curiosity.

Do you rely on fact, science, and truth to make deductions?

Does your interest in self-awareness lead to more inquiry?

More action?

Change

Are your thoughts flexible and adaptable? People who pursue improved emotional intelligence know that Fear of change can be paralyzing, posing threats to success and happiness by limiting or eliminating risk. People who seek improved emotional intelligence imagine change incrementally, with flexibility and resilience. They formulate bendable plans of action and adjust to new and unexpected things. Overall, they know they will handle any magnitude of change they encounter in their lives.

Strengths and Weaknesses

We all have strengths, skills, and abilities but are mostly average. Yet we manage to slog along. People seeking improvement in emotional intelligence don't focus only on improving emotional control; they know they're competent and struggle with others. They seek to accept these variable qualities and live contentedly with their imperfections.

Improved EI means knowing one's strengths and how to use these strengths to advantage, knowing full well that achievement is not guaranteed. Likewise, it is vital not to predetermine that you shouldn't attempt something because you believe you are weak. People seeking improvement in EI welcome challenges and risks with a balanced and open mind. People seeking improved EI know that neither failure nor success defines an individual. Failing and succeeding are never enough evidence to identify oneself as a failure or a success.

Self- and Other-Awareness

Better awareness of others builds character and is a key to EI improvement. Much of our emotional intelligence comes from self-awareness, the ability to connect with ourselves. By developing other awareness, we can perceive people beneath the surface, forming a broader, more inclusive outlook for ourselves and others. Over time, this skill makes us fairer observers and collaborators in improving the emotional intelligence not only within ourselves but the EI in others.

No Offense

When we have a fair understanding of ourselves, our strengths, weaknesses, and averages, it's difficult for someone to influence that acquired attentiveness we have for ourselves through our own observable actions. Emotionally intelligent people are self-confident, not perfect (except perfectly imperfect), and open-minded, creating tolerance for unflattering judgments. When we are open to criticism, we might find truth and a better awareness of ourselves and others. To judge a person never means defining them; instead, you define yourself.

Say No

Emotional intelligence means knowing how to exert self-control, delay gratification, and avoid impulsive action. Saying *no* to others and ourselves is a challenge for many people. When it's time to say no, people who seek improvement in emotional intelligence avoid phrases that may obscure *No. I don't think I can,* or *I'm not sure.* Saying no to a commitment that honors existing obligations allows you to fulfill them without feeling anxious, stressed, and guilty.

Mistakes

People who seek improved EI acknowledge their mistakes but do not move in with them. Emotionally intelligent people may revisit their mistakes (for information), but they do not relive the past as if watching the same movie in the same theatre every day. It takes polished self-awareness to walk this tightrope between dwelling on the past and recalling it. Dwelling causes depressive anxiety, while reflecting expands choice-making, provides options, and improves outcomes.

Expect Nothing

When someone gives you something spontaneously, without expecting anything in return, this leaves a powerful impression. People who seek improved emotional intelligence build strong relationships because they think about others equally. When you give yourself to another and expect something in return, it's a transaction, not a kind gesture. You have one eye on your activities and the other on what you'll get in return. That takes you away from the moment. You can't do your best when you have a hidden agenda.

Grudges

The negative emotions that come with holding onto a grudge initiate the stress response. An unfortunate event can send your body into F^3 mode, a survival mechanism that forces you to fight or run when faced with a real or imagined threat. This reaction is essential to your survival if the danger is imminent or actual. But if the threat is imaginary, holding onto that memory can cause your body to experience severe health consequences over time. Holding onto past slights means you're reliving the event. Reliving stressful events are real to the mind and contribute to high blood pressure and heart disease, not to mention chronic states of anger and irritability.

Living with Others

Engaging with others who don't agree or attempt to thwart our intentions can be exhausting. People with improved EI can manage their interactions with people who disagree while remaining calm and content. They can consider the disagreeing person's standpoint and find solutions and common ground using reason and patience. Even when things completely derail, emotionally intelligent people can engage fairly with others, knowing that disagreement does not define the individual. A deeper dive into our emotional intelligence improvement may reveal the potential for compassionate empathy when we take another's perspectives.

Perfection

Emotionally intelligent people won't set perfection as their target because they know it isn't achievable. Human beings, by their very nature, are fallible. We may be left with a nagging sense of failure when perfection is our goal. We may spend our time lamenting our losses, preventing us from engaging in new plans. Emotionally improving people's work toward a desired goal, regardless of its process or outcome.

Gratitude

Taking time to contemplate the present moment and what it contains can improve mood, reduce stress (particularly the hormone cortisol), and make interpersonal relationships more fulfilling. Practicing gratitude is the simplest and fastest way to build emotional strength. Expressing gratitude does not mean counting your material wealth and comparing it to your neighbor's. On the contrary, statements of gratitude using an emotional intelligence theory begin with the phrase *I am*—not *I have*.

- *I am alive at this moment.*

- *I am not sick at this moment.*

- *I am not hungry at this moment.*

- *I am loved at this moment.*

- *I can manage this moment.*

- *I am courageous at this moment.*

- *I am making flexible plans for my life at this moment.*

- *I am enough at this moment.*

Genuine gratitude reflects the moment you live, your health, and the breath in your lungs. Sincere appreciation is founded in mindfulness, in which you focus on being intensely aware of what you're sensing and feeling at the moment without interpretation or judgment. Without predicting that the next moment will not be endurable. Without being afraid.

To express gratitude for things such as a home, car, job, or family transforms gratitude into Fear, competition, and comparison. If your contentedness is attached to what you own, what you have in the bank, or what you drive, your F^3 will skyrocket for Fear of losing what you use to define your self-worth.

Can you be enough and have nothing?

Gratitude establishes its meaning from within and assesses the present moment for its foundation in truth. You must start each day believing that you are already enough, already complete, and be grateful for life alone. You can leave your attempts to improve to their outcomes—never a summation of yourself and the new version of yourself you had hoped to become.

Disconnect

Studies have shown that something as simple as a five-minute break to breathe and rest can lower stress hormone levels. Technology enables constant communication, making us available to others 24/7. Disconnecting from work, even when you're at work, can have multiple benefits. They can range from increased productivity, feeling less tired, more meaningful career and life balance, enjoying life more, being happier with your love and family, and overall great mental health.

Sleep

It's difficult to overstate the importance of sleep in increasing your emotional intelligence and managing stress hormone levels. When you sleep, your brain recharges, shuffling through the day's memories and storing or discarding them (which causes dreams) to wake up alert and clearheaded. High EI individuals know that their self-control, attention, and memory are reduced when they don't sleep. So, they make sleep a top priority.

Self-Talk

The more you ruminate on negative thoughts, the more power you give them. Most of our negative thoughts are just that—thoughts. Thoughts are facts to the mind, and the body responds to them. When it feels like something always or never happens, your brain's natural tendency is to perceive threats (inflating the frequency or severity of an event). Emotionally intelligent people separate their thoughts from the facts to escape the cycle of imagination and move toward a more rational decision-making process and outlook.

Self-Awareness and Comparison

You no longer improve your emotional intelligence when you derive self-awareness from others' opinions. While it's impossible to entirely turn off your reactions to what others think of you, you can always consider the criticisms and judgments and accept or reject them. That way, no matter what others think or do, your source for unconditional self-acceptance comes from you. At times others may make valid suggestions for your self-awareness. Regardless, you are the arbitrator of what you are willing to change or not change about yourself.

Emotional intelligence, being a creation of the mind, precisely like emotion itself, can be difficult to gauge without self-awareness and a system of comparison to others.

Am I as emotionally stable as other people?

Am I as happy as she is?

Am I as successful as that person?

Am I keeping up?

Comparisons are one way to form a baseline for where we are in life. Using comparison is a common way of assessing our pace toward our ambitions. Without comparison, an assessment of emotional intelligence isn't even possible.

Am I angrier than most people?

Should I be more or less assertive with her?

What does it mean about me that I didn't win?

Nothing alive lives alone, so comparing ourselves to something or someone is often our single reference for motivation and desire. Comparison can help or hinder our drive toward goals, achievements, and how we assess our successes and failures

Comparison can be as straightforward as wishing to be taller, thinner, or younger. It is often an assessment of our athleticism, intellect, or extroversion capabilities.

Although comparison can help articulate and establish our goals, those who regularly compare themselves to others may experience deep dissatisfaction, guilt, or remorse in themselves and their lives. They may engage in self-destructive behaviors like lying, physical aggression, disordered eating, or unnecessary surgery.

When we want to feel better about ourselves, we compare ourselves to people who are worse off. When we want to improve, though, we may compare ourselves to people higher achieving than ourselves. People generally engage in either upward or downward comparisons. We compare ourselves with those we believe are better than we imagine, resulting in insecurity and jealousy. In contrast, low comparison can result in overconfidence and arrogance. We influence our goals with comparison, but we are more likely to accept the challenge if we first accept ourselves.

We may define self-acceptance as recognizing the inherent value we hold in the very moment of our lives. From that perspective, we can acknowledge that we are already complete, already good enough and that our goals, whether we achieve them, cannot define us or interfere with our inherent human worth.

Locus (Focus) of Control

We can describe the *locus of control* as the degree to which we perceive an outcome contingent on personal action or external forces. The locus of control exists as a continuum from a more internalized orientation to a more externalized direction. For example, would you rather be the world's richest person but think you're the poorest? Or would you rather be the world's poorest person but have everyone think you're the world's most prosperous?

You can only expect to improve individual skills and abilities as you believe they would benefit your life, not people's perception of you. Much like your goal to improve your emotional intelligence.

Which, as we know, can take a lot of work.

No one ever drowned in sweat.

14

The Last Time I Killed My Father

But in the end, one needs more courage to live than to kill himself.
—Albert Camus

It can be frightening to change a storyline where we are no longer victims but adults with free will and potential. It is not unusual for me to see people kicking and screaming their way into the here and now without gripping an old plotline for comfort and adaptation.

"I'm a victim!"

"Where do you get that idea?"

"I was mistreated when I was a child."

"Is there no other way to describe yourself?"

"I am a survivor."

"Can you describe yourself from the perspective of this moment?"

"I'm a victimized survivor."

"Can you describe yourself without either of those terms?"

"No!"

"Would you like to?"

I had much the same tug of war, push, and pull with myself and my idea that I was once upon a time a victim. I was often jealous of other boys living in their family homes, especially boys who knew their biological fathers. I watched curiously as my friends and their fathers loaded station wagons for an extended family trip to South Dakota, fishing gear, baseball bats and gloves, BB guns, and suitcases. Fathers were imaginative; my memories glow like the golden trophies in front of the principal's office, where I often sat, secretly looking forward to Mr. Noel's chastising.

The first time I killed my father, I imagined him driving a red convertible with a white leather interior off a cliff into a black hole. The abyss was filled with snapping turtles, sharks, and wilder beasts—a creature I saw on *Mutual of Omaha's Wild Kingdom*. This event and subsequent inspirations for my imagination were our only activities together. Sometimes I drove, sometimes he would—just the two of us flying through the air like *Thelma and Louise*.

As I got older, I imagined a herd of buffalo stomping my father. Sometimes he was pecked by a murder of crows or abducted by translucent aliens who took him into space to examine his brain. I fantasized about the aliens returning him to the wrong planet, tossing him out as they hovered over, leaving him to wander the moon's dusty surface, only to be discovered by another race of aliens who also explored the interior of his head and found nothing. "How can a human function without a brain?" the space creatures joked and threw him out into the haze of space.

I thought, "If my father had only loved me, I would have been more successful, lovable, and worthy. I would have been an achievement!" I told myself, "A lifetime of failure is my destiny. Always second best. Never first. I have no way out. I never had a father!"

Considering I invented the idea that I *needed* my father's love to be someone special, I was left with no way to redeem myself but to wander the surface of distant planets to convince him to love me. Only then could I be whole and worthy of love from others.

I fashioned a very broken person by recalling these minimal, imaginative experiences. My mother's biased gossip, and my aunts' answers to my questions, were always prefaced with, "You will have to ask your mother, but . . ." These second and third-hand recollections shaped me into the boy I was at the time and helped create the colossal monster that occupied my mind. The pot steamed and hissed as if I had written a song in my head and rehearsed it to perfection.

The Victim's Song.

As I got older, I looked for my father in philosophy; I searched for him in biology, writing, reading, history, and psychology. I never found my father, but I did find my profession.

One of several derivatives of general psychology, specifically health psychology, examined how biological, social, and psychological (biopsychosocial) factors influence overall health and wellness. Health psychology, my educational objective, proposes that a person never has one disease. There will be a response from the physical body where there is a mental health issue. Likewise, there will always be a physical correlation if there is an emotional challenge.

The biopsychosocial model proposes that the body, mind, and environment are interrelated. According to this model, none of these factors exists in isolation but definitively leads to health and illness. It is the deep interrelation of all three components that produce an outcome.

Biopsychosocial assessment is a logical offshoot of the theory of health psychology. It is a human evaluation system that considers the biological, social, and psychological aspects of a person's existence when determining the cause of their health concerns, emotional and psychological.

My most profound awareness of the model was when I observed that thinking and perception were the primary sources of emotion. We instigate a physical response if we think anxiously, Fearfully, and depressively. If we learn to think and perceive differently, we can change how we feel about most things, improving overall physical and psychological health outcomes.

Because of its embrace of human anatomy and biology, established psychological theory, remarkably Stoic philosophy, rationalism, and its influence on emotional expression, EI theory and its roots in the biopsychosocial model suddenly became a clear path to success in helping not only myself but others.

My first and only encounter with my father was when he appeared in the obituary column of the local newspaper. On the pages of the *Brockton Enterprise* was a picture of him, a blurry, excised cut out from what seemed to be once a group picture. The image was spellbounding. Unlike the creature who lived under a bridge, I had known for many years. The obituary said his children survived him but did not name me. Others were also detailed, those who had loved him and would miss him.

My first impression was of the inevitability of death and how this event cuts short many of the things we've spent our lives lamenting.

Therapists don't often discuss death awareness with people seeking hope and positivity, so it was also a curious idea. I was intrigued by the theory proposed by German philosopher Martin Heidegger who inspired Jean-Paul Sartre and other existentialist thinkers. The concept of mortality and its role in living can lead to fulfillment rather than the desperation we feel lamenting earlier troubles.

Nobody likes to think about their eventual death, and thoughts of aging and death can unleash a heightened state of urgency in most of us. Although death can be frightening, it can also positively improve emotional intelligence.

The dominant psychological theories in use today, only until recently, assumed that contemplating our demise when we are not ill prompts depression, Fear, and F^3 and should be avoided. Literature from various fields has offered other explanations.

Positive psychology, for example, proposes that growth is possible following a traumatic event. And we can grow from adversity rather than relying on the widespread belief that trauma is always debilitating and unfortunate.

Likewise, when we fairly and reasonably incorporate life's time limitations, we can help improve focus, particularly in how much value we place on living in the moment.

We can presume that living in the moment will make taking chances more conceivable. We may, from this perspective, be more willing to engage in an adventure without certainty of its outcome. We might choose individuality over conformity and personal choice over orthodoxy. We could be empowered by the variety of options we have when the certainty of death plays a role in how we live our limited days. I recalled the years I spent wondering what it would be like to drive to my father's house and introduce myself, only to Fear his rejection and how that Fear rendered me immobile.

The older we get, the more involuntarily we become aware of death. The mirror, combined with the random comment or unexpected observation of how the years have suddenly passed, brings us reluctantly closer to the unsettling awareness that we are mortal. We realize that we can't stop life's unfolding by simply ignoring it, rushing from one place to another, getting and taking, and dashing as if it all will result in less worry and discomfort later on. None of it does but instead breeds more panic, hurrying to get things to ward off the terrible events.

Some of us, as we age, begin to focus on improving health and decluttering a knotty lifestyle, choosing to appreciate the present moment over the F^3, worry, and distress of our imagination of the future. Sadly, this awareness comes when there is likely less time to appreciate the refreshing liberation possible from accepting life's limitations and the opportunities we often postpone.

This period of life can be a highly creative time or a phase of regret, disappointment, and grief. The main factor contributing to either outcome may lie in how soon we embrace our own shelf life. We might, at this point, become more aware of what we will leave behind and what we can reasonably do—thereby transcending death as we had always expected to do.

Those seeking to perpetuate their experiences are likely to own their past and present moments. Whether producing art, raising a family, passing on family history, or helping others, leaving a legacy can help manage aging and death and produce fruit in emptiness.

The last time I killed my father, I succeeded where I had consistently failed. I stood over his open casket and looked at his nose and closed eyes. His lapel had a food stain on it as if he had just finished eating a bologna sandwich before resting in the gray-colored box.

I didn't know him except that his face was like mine. Somehow he had much more hair than I did, but his jaw was square and strong. He was missing part of a finger on his right hand. I reached up to touch my earlobes, finding that they were like his in size and shape. (My mother's earlobes were attached to her lower ear, making my father and I remarkably connected.)

People buzzed around, crying, wiping tears away, and standing somberly, folding their hands in front. Someone walked an older woman to the casket they called Mom.

Instead of killing my father that day, I accepted myself and the conditions of my life. I owned my thoughts and perceptions and the self-destructive feelings they produced. I suddenly realized I didn't need my father or anything else to have human worth. As if opening a floodgate, in place of anger, Fear, and disappointment, I put acceptance, patience, and the possibility of someday receiving a similar appraisal. I reached up to my left earlobe and smiled.

The anguish I had lived with ended—my memories suddenly reversed, leaving me to embrace the knowledge that it was never about my father and always about me and my thoughts. I no longer *needed* him as a complete condition, and I did not need him, realizing I could live much more contentedly without anything.

A miracle of DNA and technology discovered that my father had a son. I hesitated to contact him, believing I was not good enough for the son of a man I had come to think of as the All-Powerful Oz. I asked him for a picture of our father, and I got a promise but nothing else. I wondered if this stranger looked like me, and I smiled, thinking of his earlobes.

I am potentially the arbitrator of how I feel about everything I perceive because I can change my thoughts and perspectives. I work to capture my ideas, engage them with curiosity and dispute them when necessary. It may take the rest of my life, but I intend to replace my self-sabotaging beliefs with more rational, valuable, and self-improving cognitions. My daily ritual reinforces this aim. When I wake up, I believe it is a beautiful privilege to be alive, to breathe, think, appreciate, and love.

It will always be tempting to construct a convenient excuse for the less-enjoyable happenings in my life. Improvement in EI is a day-by-day process, often resulting from self-examination and curiosity, choosing celebration no matter what I find there.

Improved EI is a daily slog.

No one ever drowned in sweat.

15

White Knuckles

I feel too much. That's what's going on.' 'Do you think one can feel too much? Or just feel in the wrong ways?' 'My insides don't match up with my outsides.' 'Do anyone's insides and outsides match up?' 'I don't know. I'm only me.' 'Maybe that's a person's personality: the difference between the inside and outside.' 'But it's worse for me.' 'I wonder if everyone thinks it's worse for him.' 'Probably. But it is worse for me. —Jonathan Safran Foer, *Extremely Loud & Incredibly Close*

The expression of Fear is universally recognized. While generally considered a *negative* emotion, Fear is essential in keeping us safe, mobilizing us to overcome danger—real or imagined. Our human design uses the same brain system to resolve conflict with bears, scorpions, and skunks as it does when there's even a hint of an obstacle to our goals.

"If the stick moves, RUN!"

"The stick moved!"

"Where'd you go?"

While fight-flight-freeze (F^3) gave us an early evolutionary advantage and preserved our species for thousands of years, it is still present today. Only it serves an entirely new purpose. After years of using the Fear response to improve our odds of physical survival, we now use our F^3 principally to manage the threats produced by our imagination.

You might hear, "You're no good!"

"How dare you say that to me!" is the typical comeback, "I think we're supposed to fight now."

"I'm new to speaking the truth."

"OK, well, you're bald!"

"Can't fight about that. You're right!"

"We've been honoring our lies for too long."

"Should we fight?"

"Probably."

"What would people say if we didn't?"

We no longer face sabertoothed tigers or their modern-day equivalent while washing the laundry or frying an egg. Preparing for an encounter with a wolf in the grocery store would be extraordinarily unusual. We often run into traffic jams, unexpected parking tickets, and people who refuse to use their turning signals. Each offense tells F^3 that we will be unreasonably inconvenienced and need immediate protection.

The areas of the brain that instigate the F^3 response are precisely the same as in our ancestors' brains 15,000 years ago. Once, our survival meant that we had to remember where the buffalo roamed (retrospective thought) and what those clouds meant about where we would sleep (anticipatory thinking). Instead of using these brain operations for adaptive living, we now use anticipatory thinking and reflection to create imagined obstacles, mythical monsters, and barriers to our goals that have very little to do with our survival.

The places where we store our memories and the structures activated when we imagine the future and reimagine the past are unchanged. The hippocampus, the cortex, and the medial temporal lobe help coordinate our depressive response to recollecting the past. In contrast, the anticipation of the future includes the prefrontal and medial temporal lobes and more posterior regions, such as the retrosplenial cortex. Studies have found a striking overlap between these brain regions.

The F^3 response is not entirely useless in modern life. It is handy for when pirates attack our cruise ship, or a burglar enters our house through a window. Otherwise, we live in a world where the usefulness of the F^3 response has significantly waned. The optimal use of the F^3 in modern living is for motivation, influencing goal setting, tempering our drive for over-reproduction, and keeping us on time. In today's world, we rarely rely on the limbic system (F^3) to prepare us for predators.

In place of a real threat, people often use their idle time to immerse themselves in thoughts of uncertainty and dread conjured from memories of the past or imaginations of the future. They live day-to-day in F^3, picturing some impending catastrophe or reimagining something that has already happened and may happen again.

I remember when a bumblebee flew through the front door, chasing the mailman. "Oh no!" he shouted, "Get it away." He flailed his hands.

"Just swat it with your magazine," I suggested, half-hoping he wouldn't hit it. The bee seemed to have a bead on the mailman, targeting execution. "He must sense your Fear," I added, "Don't show him you're afraid."

"I'm not afraid! I don't like these damn things," he said, breathing rapidly and shallowly, "There's a nest. I'm sure of it!"

The mailman did survive the bumblebee blitz, and the bee flew away peacefully. The mailman activated his F^3, believing that he would be feeling (future focus) the sting of the kamikaze bee and that there would be more later. As he left, he remarked, "This place is dangerous. I think there's a nest around here. I will come through the back from now on." The same thinking is often applied to losing a job, a mate or partner, or a traffic jam. We express intolerance to frustration in degrees, using different words to describe the degree, i.e., depression, jealousy, guilt, and grief—each a degree of Fear.

When the mind tries to predict the future and creates a negative projection about something that hasn't and may not happen, we experience F^3 through anticipation of the answer. Most of us have experienced this tentative mindset. We instinctually want to have control of everything that touches our lives and demand certainty in every event and outcome, even when 100% confidence in the result isn't possible.

In the absence of facts, we imagine them.

Personality, learning, and reactiveness to uncertainty to real or imagined threats play essential roles in the degree of F^3 we express. Some people are neurologically less tolerant of vagueness and ambiguity and quickly respond when confronted with it. They may react with tremendous anticipatory F^3, often imagining the worst possible outcome when making plans for a future that is not guaranteed. They endlessly worry, stimulating the brain's Fear center (amygdala) and setting off the body's physiological responses to terrifying, imaginative thoughts (sympathetic nervous system).

Nature does not preprogram humans to Fear anything. We learn to worry about real and imagined threats as we grow and develop. Brain imaging studies suggest that we learn to Fear something by reminding ourselves of an unpleasant, disturbing experience and predict every potential harm disproportionately. We form neural pathways around the Fearful thought, and it takes root. The body responds to the frightening thought viscerally (sweating, increased heart rate), causing neurons to strengthen their connections, thickening the branches, and, over time, making everything less flexible.

We acquire our Fears over time, through experience, primarily between birth and twelve years old. Theorists propose this is the most suitable time for the brain to align the concepts of good, bad, better, best, friend, foe, right, and wrong. This timeline for learning our Fears may coincide with our emerging drive for individuality and gaining confidence as we engage in tribal living without supervision.

As we grow and develop, the area of our brain that processes our acquired Fears, the limbic system, and the places in the cerebral cortex that store them grip like a fist everything we have ever learned to Fear and hold onto it tightly.

Nature designed that portion of our brain to identify and store information about what to Fear and alert us when we encounter something similar. Our brain lets nothing pass as we acquire Fears even remotely threatening. For example, some learn to Fear fish, fungi, or rattlesnakes, while some avoid Ferris wheels, bobcats, plaid fabric, or balloons. There is no rhyme or reason to gather the reasoning we use for the things we Fear.

"The kids made fun of me today. They said I had freckles and was ugly, and now they don't like me." This event may start our grip on Fearing freckles, blemishes, ridicule, etc. Our vice-like hold on these ideas begins to shape as we encounter related events or reimagine the initial incident. As a result, we may become overly sensitive to criticism, not our physical appearance, critical of shortcomings in others, or even tolerant of being disliked.

Mockery, sexuality, joblessness, failing, intelligence, athleticism, masculinity and femininity (gender), social class, and the fullness of our hair can represent our grips on Fear. None of these ideas are genuinely dodgy enough to rely on F^3. But we often grab hold of frightening thoughts and clamp down as if forgetting would put us in extreme danger.

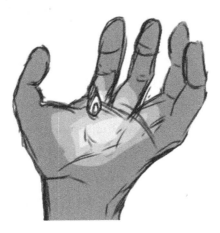

Nature allows us to store information about what *Not to Fear* (R^3), transferring Fearful data from one place in our brains to another less-fearful region.

R^3 promotes rest, renewal, and recovery.

Though easy to grab what we Fear, it isn't easy to loosen the grip on Fear. It can take seconds to grab hold of Fear, but once you've convinced your brain's Fear center to release the grasp, it can sometimes take more strength than we know to free the F^3 and exchange it for R^3. Unless we do something new, flip the script, and modify our character, our hold on these Fearful ideas grows firmer over time, weakening but never eliminating our ability to learn something new.

Emotional intelligence improvement depends on this system of cross-pollination between F^3 and R^3. Brain plasticity, the brain's inherent ability to change shape when prompted, prodded, or coerced, is a cornerstone of improving emotional intelligence.

We can work toward loosening our grip on most things we Fear. Of course, we should continue to Fear most lions, wolves, and skunks, but otherwise, we can set free almost everything else.

Loosening the Grip—An Exercise

- Please close your eyes and imagine only your breath as it causes your chest to rise and fall (approximately one minute).
- After a minute, with your eyes closed, move your thoughts to the interior of your mind. Curiously examine its structures and function.
- Look around as long as you like. Say hello to the Boss.
- Take three deep breaths and open your eyes when you're ready.
- Make a fist.
- Hold out your fist and observe it.
- Squeeze lightly.
- Imagine that inside this grip is something you Fear. Start with something easy, i.e., acne, short money, or a floundering relationship.
- Focus your eyes on the grip. Feel your grip on this Fear.
- Move your eyes to something distant, e.g., a clock on the far wall, a speck on the ceiling, or a crack in the window.

- As a stream of consciousness, while staring into the distance, say aloud everything that could go wrong if your Fear did happen, predicting what could go wrong—foretelling failure. Try to find even the most remote consequence of holding onto your Fear. If you repeat your thoughts, that's fine.

Each time you describe your distress, squeeze your fist tighter. For example:

If my hair fell out, people wouldn't like me. (Squeeze). If my hair fell out, people would laugh at me. (Squeeze). If my hair fell out, people would think I was old. (Squeeze). If my hair fell out and people thought I was old, I would have no human value. (Squeeze). I would be alone if my hair fell out and I had no human value. (Squeeze). If my hair fell out and I were alone, I would be lonely. (Squeeze). If my hair fell out and I were lonely, I would be depressed. (Squeeze). I would be hopeless if my hair fell out. Then I would be depressed. (Squeeze). If my hair fell out and I were useless, I would die. (Squeeze). If my hair fell out and I died, I wouldn't need hair. (Squeeze).

- Move your eyes to your palm, open it, and observe its emptiness.
- While continuing your gaze at your palm, inhale profoundly, and exhale in the direction of your palm until you cannot force another molecule of air from your lungs.
  - You may repeat this exercise three times before continuing with your other activities.
  - Later, pick a time to assess your behaviors against your predictions, during which you can consistently perform the exercise. For example, *I lose my hair, but people don't notice.*

Although this exercise may not immediately rid you of your Fears, if you do it often, you will find that your grip has loosened, and your worries are more manageable.

Suppose we believe we will face some skill test, ability assessment, or challenge. A final examination, running a distance and time, or posing for a photograph can illustrate these events.

We may rely on our experiences with such challenges and discern from our memory if it's something to Fear or Fear—Not. Our physical response (F^3) to the proposed challenge would reveal the intensity of our grip on the imagined Fearful event and its equally fantastical consequence. Without a specific event that matches the one we face, we may somehow engage our memories of similar events and connect them to prepare ourselves. We may feel a sudden dread over being judged, quickly discovering our many grips. We might rely on this exercise to help manage the F^3 and loosen the grip permanently.

The human imagination is endless, and so are the possible consequences we prepare ourselves to encounter even before the event occurs.

"I'm going to lose my job."

"What will happen then?"

"I'd be a failure."

"Then what."

"I fail at any job I ever have in the future."

"What would that look like?"

"My life is finished."

"Not yet. You still have twenty-one seconds left. What would you like to do with the rest of this moment we're sharing?"

Improving EI depends on exchanging Fear for FearNot.

No one ever drowned in sweat.

16

Fear—F^3

Emotions, in my experience, aren't covered by single words. I don't believe in "sadness," "joy," or "regret." Maybe the best proof that the language is patriarchal is that it oversimplifies feeling. I'd like to have complicated hybrid emotions, Germanic train-car constructions like "the happiness that attends disaster" or "the disappointment of sleeping with one's fantasy." I'd like to show how "intimations of mortality brought on by aging family members" connect with "the hatred of mirrors that begins in middle age." I'd like a word for "the sadness inspired by failing restaurants" and "the excitement of getting a room with a minibar." I've never had the right words to describe my life, and now that I've entered my story, I need them more than ever.
—Jeffrey Eugenides, *Middlesex*

Fear is a powerful emotion that plays an essential role in our survival. Fear is activated through anticipatory thought and is the prompt for activation of the F^3. Fear must have an *imaginary* component to engage it. For instance, if a bear were to walk into your room, it would not be the bear that would instigate the F^3. It would be your imagination of what the bear would do if you didn't run. Our human design is not to sit and wonder if a bear is friendly or dangerous.

We prepare for F^3 at the slightest suspicion of danger.

When in F^3, muscles tense, the heart rate and respiration increase, and our minds become alert, priming our bodies to either run from the danger or stand and fight. F^3 is a whole-body response to a real or imagined threat. We can observe the signs of F^3 in how we control our facial expressions, e.g., widening the eyes and pulling back the chin. We open our mouths wide and show our teeth. Speaking becomes more difficult. Screaming is much easier because our brain responds to threats preferring the F^3 over rational thinking. We may experience rapid breathing and higher blood pressure as we prepare to fight, flee, or freeze, flailing our arms and heading for the hills.

Overcoming the faulty use of the F^3 in response to magical thought is the ambition of emotional intelligence improvement. We might call this F^3 response *anticipatory thinking*. This use of the $F^{3,}$ when our imagination controls our current moment, is self-defeating and maladaptive. For example, we often refer to awkwardness in social situations as *social anxiety*. EI views this phrasing as a disguise. Social anxiety doesn't exist, except when we use the terminology to describe our mindset.

EI rejects the idea that social circumstance causes anxiety. Instead, EI favors the notion that the thoughts *about* the situation produced the anxiety. EI suggests that this stress results from Fear of being ridiculed, criticized, and failing—fear of imperfection and its disastrous consequences. So, the anxiety is not a product of the situation but results from the imagined perception that criticism, failure, and being poorly judged in a social situation are life-threatening.

When we use labels like social anxiety to disguise our worries, Fears, and doubts, we can never get to the issue's root. Using this notion as a path toward self-understanding, we can examine our thoughts about what *could* happen in a group rather than believing it is the group that causes the F^3 activation.

What if I say something wrong?

What if I'm not witty? Intelligent? Good-looking?

What if I'm at a loss for words and don't have something to say?

What if everything I imagined happened?

We may find comfort in addressing these anticipatory questions head-on: *What is the statistical probability that I will be the laughingstock of the party? Where is the proof that I will collapse if I can't answer a simple or complicated question? How would it be a problem if I said I don't know? How likely will I be responsible for carrying out every conversation? Where is the proof that I have to be perfect when encountering a group of people? Where is the evidence that I have to be liked by everyone I meet?*

We cannot answer these future-focused questions because the answers are only available after the experience. Then we will have valuable data to answer the questions plaguing our imagination.

We know only one thing for sure about the future. Unless you are wrestling a wildebeest, you will not likely bleed, limp, or die after facing your Fearful thoughts of the future and what it holds. You can, instead, seek evidence for what you imagine. Using this process, you will perhaps learn that you are at least average in carrying a conversation. You may discover that where there are two people, there is almost always some easy banter between them. There's only one way to find out, but believing your Fear results from social engagements will not produce practical, resourceful skill-building.

Some people seek out situations that instigate F^3. Extreme sports and other thrills can be Fear-inducing. Repeated exposure to F^3 can lead to familiarity and acclimation, reducing the effects of the F^3 in imagined situations. (Yes, even your imagined death is not as you imagine it. Fearing death needs life and can lead to the anticipatory Fear of death. *Wanting* life can be much more relaxing, rewarding, and less expensive. Wanting over needing can be the difference between living in F^3 and R^3 (rest, renewal, and recovery). Simple use of words can change most things.) Those who choose not to fly off a cliff or walk across hot coals to face their Fear can engage in a therapeutic custom known as the *shame attack*.

Shame-attacking is an exercise where the individual chooses to do something publicly that would possibly (even likely) draw attention or disapproval from others. The shame attack doesn't have to be too big or outrageous. We can start small and incrementally learn that the experience, particularly the generated self-talk, is a valuable resource for overcoming the false activation of F^3:

- Tie a long red ribbon around a banana and take it through the neighborhood. Introduce it to your friends as your new dog.
- Ride a crowded elevator standing backward (facing the rear).
- Yell out five successive stops in the subway or on the bus.
- Stand in a restaurant and sing the *Star-Spangled Banner*.

- Find a restaurant that offers two eggs in any style and ask your waiter for one fried and one boiled.

I once bought a candy bar with a hundred-dollar bill at a grocery store, returned it five times, and paid using a new one-hundred-dollar bill. I danced on the sidewalk in front of Caesar's Palace, stood on the street corner with a tip cup, and read *The Catcher in the Rye* aloud. (I made $6.83.) I was overwhelmed with self-doubt and shame each time, but I endured it, and I am better at engaging with groups, often to the point of being too loud—yet another opportunity for a shame attack. I ran each experience through the ABCs and successfully confronted my self-limiting self-talk.

When we believe others may judge our performance, the shame attack aims to help overcome the caustic thoughts we feed ourselves. We must investigate the broader objective of the exercise. It is recommended not for busy EI work but to help those who experience self-destructive, Fearful thoughts in situations where evaluation and comparison are components of imagination. We must overcome, surpass and get entirely away from the F^3 that keeps us from living fully, exposed as imperfect.

Some researchers have suggested humans only possess three emotional potentials, e.g., we are afraid (F^3), we aren't sure (freeze), or we are not afraid (R^3).

Emotional intelligence theory supports the idea that people are in F^3 (fear) or R^3 (FearNot) throughout the day. EI proposes that emotions, mainly F^3, cannot be practically understood if we use imprecise emotive language, i.e., depression, anger, jealousy, and guilt, to describe our state of mind. For example, if we define our emotional mindset as *depressed*, we would not be likely to explore the wealth of psychological information hidden behind that word. Instead, we may express that we are afraid—significantly afraid.

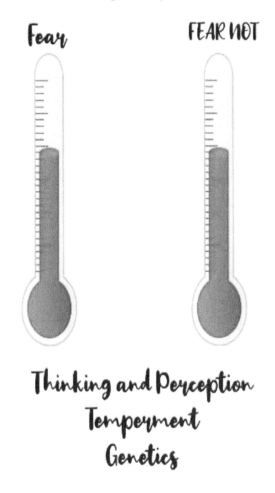

EI regards depression, anger, and jealousy as three of the highest degrees of F^3 Fear humans can express. We can't get to the thought-based roots of our emotional expression if we use vague conceptual language to describe our state of mind. Expressive language is replete with nuance, impression, and shade.

Describing a mindset as depression, anger, or jealousy is like wearing a mask over the emotional state. When we view emotional imbalance as some *degree* of Fear, we can explore our options for improvement from that perspective. For example: "How are you feeling today?"

"I'm depressed."

"That's terrible. What's going on?"

"My landlord will evict me, and I will be homeless."

"Gracious! Are you packed yet?"

"No, she hasn't notified me yet. I just heard about it downstairs in the laundry room. I'm sure she will let me know soon."

"Why are they doing this to you?"

"I don't think they like me."

"Those bastards. You're a wonderful person!"

"I'm no good."

"No! You're an amazing person! You're handsome and intelligent, successful, and everyone loves you!"

Instead of the word *depression* to mask what is truly happening inside the mind, we may use the word Fear:

"How are you thinking today?"

"I'm too depressed to think."

"What are you thinking about?"

"I'm going to be evicted."

"How do you know?"

"I heard about it in the laundry room this morning."

"What are you so afraid of?"

"Homelessness."

"Is that likely?"

"It's just more crap to manage."

"What are you afraid of?"

"My life is a hole."

"What is a hole?"

"You know what I mean."

"Why don't you tell me."

We disguise expressions of F^3 behind abstract words and vague images, e.g., guilt, grief, and frustration, thereby preventing emotional problem-solving at its root. Additionally, when a helper is involved, two distinct conversations are likely to occur without defining the emotional term in some familiar detail for both the helper and beneficiary, leading to misunderstanding. If we call depression the biggest Fear, we can better explore what leads to what sustains it and the F^3:

"A hole is a dark place with no doors or windows."

"Yet there are two windows and a door in this room."

"I feel like I can't get out."

"You certainly can get out. Stand up and go."

"I have nowhere to go."

"Where would you go if you chose to stand?"

"I'd go back and do it all over again."

"Would you do it all perfectly the second time?"

"I'd damn well try."

"Did you try the first time around?"

"I thought I did, but not hard enough to please everyone else."

"Wouldn't you face the same opposition if you could travel back in time?"

"I don't know. I'm willing to try."

"Are you willing to live in the moment you are occupying instead?"

"No, I'm a failure at this moment."

"What are you so desperately afraid of?"

"I'm a failure."

"Prove it."

When we believe we are helpless, primarily due to our imagination of what could or might happen (rarely what is happening), the limbic system goes into a Fear state by predicting the future and provoking action—the fantasy increases the intensity of the Fear. The amygdala turns on areas essential for the motor functions of fighting, freezing in place, or fleeing. Identifying strategies for coping with potential obstacles, comfort, and balance reduces the intensity of the Fear and can establish a sturdy framework for engaging in *FearNot*.

The degrees of (F^3) Fear and (R^3) FearNot are given names, the luxury of spoken language:

- *Depression* (high Fear): I'm afraid I'm no good. I'm afraid I am a loser. I'm afraid I have no purpose in life. I'm afraid I am a complete and utter loser.

- *Anger* (big Fear): I'm afraid I am not getting what I should. I am afraid I am not getting what I must. I am afraid I am not getting what I have to have. I am worried I am not getting what I need.

- *Jealousy* (high Fear): I am afraid I don't have what he has. I am afraid I am no good if I don't have what that woman has around her neck. I am afraid I am no good if I don't have his car, house, hair, job, and dog.

- *Guilt* (excessive Fear): I am afraid I made a mistake and am not supposed to make mistakes. I am worried that I cannot take back my mistake. I'm so scared I am stuck with my mistakes forever, and now I can never be good again.

- *Grief* (manageable Fear): I am afraid I will miss that person, place, or thing. I'm afraid it will be a painful adjustment, but I will likely handle it.

- *Frustration* (measured Fear): I am afraid I am inconvenienced and cannot stand it. I am so scared I have lost that thirty minutes of my life forever, but I will likely handle it.

- *Sadness* (low Fear): I'm afraid I will live in a world where things I'm not particularly eager to happen will happen, but I will likely handle it.

Without words, we would speak primarily with our faces, limited to expressions of pleasure and displeasure in degrees. Our facial expressions of F^3 can be interpreted as anger, revealing frown lips and cheeks; an indication of pressure may include darting eyes and a swiveling head, as people presumably try to see and hear better in an environment that might be threatening.

Imagine, for example, you encounter a man at a train station, and he is crying, standing by the edge of the train tracks.

"What is wrong? Can I help?"

"Ich habe meinen Koffer verloren."

"Do you need something?"

"Mein Mittagessen war in meinem Koffer."

We might rub our eyes and point at our hearts. We might take the man by the arm and guide him back to the station house. We might sigh when he walks toward the tracks. We might look him in the eyes and express Fear of standing too close to the train tracks.

"Please come back. I'm afraid."

"Lassen Sie mich allein! Meine Frau bringt mir ein Sandwich," at which point you might call the police.

Likewise, even when we speak the same language, misunderstandings are easy when we rely on words to describe our emotional state.

We cannot use our faces to express jealousy or embarrassment—only degrees of displeasure. Likewise, we cannot use only our faces to communicate contentment, love, or empathy—only degrees of pleasure. While language allows a more precise explanation of our thoughts, we often lose the precision of interpretation and meaning, even with words, when we steer too far away from F^3 and R^3.

After all, we only perceive the words and how we use them to understand them from another's perspective.

We often refer to persistent F^3 as stress, anxiety, or nervousness. Using these words to describe our state of mind prevents us from finding a solution to what we Fear. We will forever identify the emotion rather than its source from this perspective. The inability to identify the base from which the discomfort comes, referring to it as frustration rather than Fear, prevents us from distinguishing solutions from concepts.

>"I'm so angry I could spit."
>
>"You look pretty worked up."
>
>"That woman was so condescending."
>
>"What happened?"
>
>"She talked to me like I was her dog."
>
>"What makes it a problem for you?"
>
>"It's not nice."
>
>"How should she treat you?"
>
>"She should treat me with respect."
>
>"What do you think it means about you when you're not treated respectfully?"
>
>"That I'm not worthy of respect."
>
>"What are you so afraid of?"

If we believe we need the respect of others to reason that we are respectable, then we will use the F^3 in every encounter that communicates otherwise. On the other hand, if we believe we are acceptable as we are (R^3) and have the support of others (R^3), we may live more contentedly in the moment.

Nature's intent for F^3 was to help us reduce or avoid risks of death or serious bodily injury. We never or rarely ever encounter such dangers. But we are wired to perceive a threat, even when the perception is inaccurate, even when it has no identifiable cause for alarm other than our imagination of what could happen next. We no longer engage with our environment to determine risk but instead use faulty, self-destructive perceptions.

We will return to our Fear and FearNot model in the next chapter. At this juncture, it will be necessary to know that we are all designed to engage in obstacles to our goals similarly, to some degree. We can use compassion, empathy, sympathy, and patience toward those we Fear or meet Fear with more Fear. When you know that others are operating from the same place of Fear, you may improve your perception and response to it.

That will take much more work than most people are used to improve EI.

No one ever drowned in sweat.

17

FearNot

Breath is the bridge that connects life to consciousness, which unites your body with your thoughts. Use your breath to retake hold of your mind whenever your mind becomes scattered. —Thich Nhat Hanh

Once we can manage the body, the mind can provide an abundance of rational, proof-based thinking. This activity prompts the R^3 response to release feel-good hormones, including dopamine and serotonin, slowing the heart rate, lowering blood pressure, and strengthening the immune system to fight disease through nerve and hormonal signals.

As with our previous chart showing the Fear response, we can illustrate the FearNot reaction in the same way:

Fear

Depression
Anger
Jealousy
Guilt
Grief
Frustration
Sadness

FEAR NOT

Contentment
Love
Altruism
Empathy
Collaboration
Cooperation
Joint Attention
Pointing
Curiosity
Matching/Normal
Copying

Thinking and Perception
Temperament
Genetics

- *Contentment* (Highest FearNot): Contentment is the highest degree of having FearNot. To be content, one must *accept* all things, which does not mean we should *like* all things. Only that everything is how it should be. We can endeavor to change things, but to attempt to change what exists using Fear will likely alienate, distance, separate, and cause F^3. Being content can also help distinguish between *wants* and *needs*.

When we are content, we may be more present in the exact location of mindfulness. When we are satisfied, the abundance of the present is enough to lead to Fearlessness, knowing that to live peacefully means we cannot derive joy from getting and keeping material things.

- *Love* (High FearNot): Emotional intelligence theory defines love as having FearNot of others, particularly an intimate partner. Healthy intimate relationships involve those who are mutually responsive to each other without compromising a sense of self. We can live contentedly with others by recognizing, understanding, and supporting each person's authority to oversee their own lives while partnering with others. This challenge is more difficult when engaging in a mutual relationship where acceptance of individuality is a lifetime challenge. When unconditional acceptance isn't possible, we are afraid and not in an association founded on love.

- *Altruism* (High FearNot): Altruism is when we act to promote someone else's welfare, even at risk or cost to ourselves.

- *Empathy* (High FearNot): Empathy is the ability to sense other people's emotions and imagine what someone else might think or feel. Similarly, we can express compassion and sympathy when we cannot honestly share the experience but strongly connect with others. The problem does not have to be fundamental to know that it is honest to someone else.

- *Collaboration/Cooperation* (Medium FearNot): Collaboration and cooperation mean working with another person or group to achieve or do something.

- *Joint Attention* (Moderate FearNot): When one person purposefully coordinates their attention with another person. Joint attention involves at least two people paying attention to the same thing, intentionally and for social reasons.

- *Pointing* (FearNot): Pointing is often a pre-verbal communication and seems to be in our human nature. We instinctively extend an index finger when people draw attention to something. This gesture has been observed across the globe, suggesting that it's a universal human impulse, perhaps like yawning or laughing.

- *Curiosity* (FearNot): Open and curious people orient their lives around appreciating novelty and a strong urge to explore, discover, and grow.

- *Matching/Normal* (FearNot): Matching is an essential skill helping to improve many cognitive abilities like visual memory, short-term memory, and pattern recognition. Matching also helps with focus.

- *Copying* (FearNot): Even at a very young age, we imitate behavior. Caregiver behavior presents powerful lessons to a child and leaves impressions on the developing mind. Children store both positive and negative images in their minds to imitate or test later.

The lower-hanging fruits on this chart are the remedial characteristics of human development and, if not present, should be built stronger to endure the weight of the fruits often out of reach for many. We might spend more time with the concepts of Contentment, Love, and Empathy as they are the highest states of FearNot.

To be content means that we accept things as they are but do not render us powerless to do something by contrast. On the contrary, we are likely to engage in better problem-solving with others and ourselves, lessening the urgency and magnitude of what we think we need to live contentedly to what we would instead want to live.

Contentedness is the expression of the *I*, where unconditional acceptance of self must precede all emotional challenges. When we can accept our definition of *I* – our flaws, weaknesses, averages, and strengths and know contrary opinions, e.g., criticism, disapproval, and ridicule can be withstood, we can accept others using the same fairness of evaluation.

Love is the unconditional acceptance of another and is an expression of *We*. Emotional intelligence theory proposes that the potential of establishing an intimate partnership is limited unless the I can exist entirely. Too often, people in partnerships claim that their companion *completes* them or *makes* them *what they are. I couldn't live without him!* These positions reveal a weakness in the *I* and cannot withstand time. Companionships shaped around these magical ideas are products of neediness, desperation, and Fear.

Empathy, Compassion, and Sympathy are expressions of connectedness to others and define the concept of *Us*. Our frame of reference cannot be from personal experience to have a developed sense of us. The idea of *Us* is to accept that we do not have to share the same experience as others to feel connected to them or the experience.

We cannot reasonably state that it is false *because it doesn't happen to me*. I hope to continue in the traditions of human collaborative, cooperative society, the framework of human survival.

Our emotional lives will be much more durable when we can claim an unconditional acceptance of ourselves, our companions, and the world. From this foundation, hope will live like the pear that grows from the limb of an apple tree.

It will take the strength of will to do this.

No one ever drowned in sweat.

18

Emotionless

The moment we cry in a film is not when things are sad but
when they turn out to be more beautiful than we expected them to be.
—Alain de Botton

Emotionlessness may result from not managing overwhelming thoughts of betrayal, disappointment, or other unpleasant events. While being emotionless is, in fact, an emotion, EI theory endorses the use of emotional constraint employing rational thought, as it is supportive of health under the circumstances of the moment. Being impulsive, angry, depressed, or thoughtless and behaving in ways that bring despair to ourselves and others is not adaptive to healthy human life and social living and should be forcefully encountered.

While healthy people can sometimes benefit from appearing emotionless in certain situations, it is by no means the default state for those who seek to improve their EI. Improvement requires evaluation, restructuring, and even replacing the mind's well-rehearsed language with our more functional internal dialogue.

Our internal narrative, or how we talk to ourselves inside our heads, presents certain limitations to self-expression. We can achieve that goal when we use words to express our thoughts. Sometimes, however, we hit a roadblock in how far our words can go to express our thoughts, leaving us speechless and turning to more primitive modes of communication. We often see people rendered speechless when addressing the unexpected circumstances of life. Silence, distance, and uncommunicativeness are forms of communication that words cannot express. Depression and anger, for example, are depths of emotional expression that words cannot seem to reach.

Broadly, humans cannot always express all they think using spoken language's established perimeters. Emotion may then rely on linking the mind to all available forms of expression, ranging from clearly spoken thought to total silence, the point at which no words can replace what we think is better than a shoe hitting a plate-glass window. Emotion, it appears, is a design of nature intended to add breadth and dimension to our encounters with others.

Language may be its buffer.

Our thoughts profoundly shape the expression of emotions and are central to our human experience. We rely on self-talk (psycholinguistics) to explore our truth—the rules we use to regulate acceptable and unacceptable. Our self-talk is the arbitrator of what we believe to be good, bad, terrible, better, awful, and best. Identifying our self-talk and hearing our private dialogue with our minds can be described as the absolute epicenter of human emotional expression.

Even with the supreme force of absolute will, a well-established internal language can endure even after achieving intellectual insight. Of course, many factors, both gross and granular, are related to the expression of emotion. However, we can imagine self-talk as the cork in a bottle of champagne; the instigation of emotional expression activated even before identifying the activating thought. Nevertheless, self-talk precedes emotional expression and can be identified, isolated, and improved.

For most of us, the mind's emotional language represents our individualized version of reality, a time-tested set of rules for what we will and will not accept in ourselves and others. Most of us sanction what we say inside our heads as indisputable facts and leave our thoughts as they have been relatively unchallenged for a lifetime.

Much like the expanse of a well-furnished home, our minds contain broken pieces and tattered fabric that, no matter how much effort we put into it, will never be helpful or safe to keep around. Emotional intelligence theory focuses on our self-talk and how we concentrate on the rubbish of our minds to furnish our thoughts. EI improvement hopes to shake off the cobwebs of our well-rehearsed self-talk and rearrange the furniture of our minds, starting with a reassessment of what we construe as *truth*.

Debilitative, self-destructive, and maladaptive self-talk is often the nucleus of frustration, anger, vengeance, social distancing, and violence. It carries a myriad of parallel and equally undermining health problems. More adaptive self-talk can help produce and maintain better health outcomes. Reassessing maladaptive thoughts, like reexamining that two-legged stool you've kept in the corner all these years and couldn't bear to throw away, is likely one of the primary obstacles to achieving your goal of improved emotional intelligence.

We want to hold on to things!

But only until we have a more valued replacement.

Enriched emotional intelligence will depend on managing thought, self-talk, and a fact-based evaluation system. The simple question is, *Is it true?* Or *Can I prove what I tell myself?* can go a long way to rearranging the furniture of your mind.

EI theory does not endorse *positive* thinking as an alternative to factual, rational thought. Positive thinking is magical reasoning that places an upbeat, optimistic spin on the future. We often use positive thinking to influence the imagined outcome of a future event.

The downside of positive thinking comes when the optimistic predictions we imagine about the future do not work or do not materialize, as is often the case. To that end, not only are we left with managing the realized, tangible outcome, but we often turn on ourselves, believing we are unlucky and victims of unfairness.

"I thought positively, and everything went to hell in a hand-wagon anyway. It must be me, and I have had no luck. The rest of my life will be luckless, and what I do or think, it will all go to mush."

Likewise, we often use *negative* thoughts to predict failure, using the past as evidence of future outcomes. By failing, we can claim to have expected it and, therefore, be less problematic. If we succeed, we view it as a fluke or a temporary benefit, an unreliable and fleeting event.

Negative and positive thinking gives certainty to uncertain things, using imagination or fallible memory of the past as indicators of what to expect.

We cannot reliably predict the future, rendering both positive and negative self-talk useless fabrications of the mind.

We place ourselves at a disadvantage by relying on these dynamic management systems. For example, if we were to think, "Tomorrow will be better than today," several unfortunate and fundamentally observable results can occur. First, tomorrow does not have to be better than today for you to live contentedly with the moment; now, tomorrow, and yesterday cannot be the conditions you accept.

There is no reliable process for predicting tomorrow, or that you will even be around to engage with it. It may be more emotionally intelligent to be with the moment of your life and accept it entirely as if you had chosen it yourself. Likewise, you may develop a more manageable mindset, knowing that you will handle tomorrow just as you have managed every other day of your life.

The past is also not a reliable source for predicting the future. The past is unique and cannot share every similarity with the future to make it wholly reliable for prediction. The past is not an unfailing resource of accuracy and truth. We can believe that each time we reimagine our personal history, we change it somehow, rendering our memory of the past wholly unreliable for the purposes for which we are using it.

While we are sitting, anticipating the future, using positive and negative thoughts, and reliving the past, we imagine ferocious dragons and the imaginary scenarios we will use to avoid our lives' fundamental, irretrievable moments. Even more damaging, we use twenty percent of our stored energy to manage a threat that does not exist, leaving our immune system vulnerable and weakened, lacking precious resources to fight actual danger and potential disease.

I have always told the most hardened, F^3-ridden people (at the most opportune moment) that their problems are entirely imaginary. "If you could describe your problems without using the past or the future, what problems would you have?" Only the keenest listener responds, "I wouldn't have any problems."

Most people answer this question by drawing on some aspects of the past and quickly imagining the future. "I am afraid of catching COVID-19," they might say. "I'm afraid my mother will catch it. I'm afraid I won't get my job back. I'm afraid my wife will leave me because we are together so much, and she's sick of me."

"Be in this moment," I say. "What is happening right now?"

"Right now?" They often look perplexed. "Shouldn't I prepare?"

"For what," I ask.

"For everything!"

"Sure," I say, "You can make flexible plans about what you can do if you have the virus or how you can manage not getting it. But if you terrorize yourself, you will complicate your life to the point where you can't live it. You will be anxious, thinking that your life will be over if you get the virus and you will not recover. You can take reasonable precautions and make flexible plans; otherwise, you cannot imagine every inevitability. It's as if a mountain lion is chasing you around your mind all day."

"I'm not sure how to stop doing that."

"When there is nothing you can do," I say, "Do nothing."

"I have to be prepared!"

"For what?" I ask, "You can't handle anything that isn't in the present. Make flexible plans. That's all you can do." I pause. "Make sure even your flexible plans are flexible. There is no way to predict the future and every outcome without making yourself insane."

We often enmesh our thoughts with our imagination, so interlaced with the past and the future that we prevent ourselves from accepting the present moment and its potential for offering a life less stressful and more contented.

If we continue to imagine dragons, the mind's frustrations will likely be unchanged tomorrow or next week and compounded by time and other maladaptive prospects.

Of course, we can make adaptable plans, but nothing can be guaranteed when the entire equation is otherwise unknown. Regardless of the outcome, it may be best to rely on current facts.

There is no promise that you will like everything you may eventually handle, but you will take everything you encounter for the rest of your life, as you always have.

The simplest method I have ever used to disengage myself from predicting the future, to reduce or eliminate my imagined F^3, is to ask myself: *What are your problems without using the past or the future to describe them? Where is the proof that you will not handle whatever happens in the future? You're in the future now, handling everything you Feared.*

Without anticipating the future or reliving the past, I focus on the magnitude of unappreciated possibilities available in the present moment.

Unless the present moment includes a man with a knife or a vicious, rabid chipmunk, imagination is primarily responsible for the problems we think we have. A stronger sense of the present moment is one of the primary ingredients of improved emotional intelligence. We can awaken to the fact that we have no problems without our imagination provoking them.

That may be a challenging goal.

No one ever drowned in sweat.

19

If You Can Feel It, You Can Heal It

No live organism can continue for long to exist sanely under conditions of absolute reality; even larks and katydids are supposed, by some, to dream. —Shirley Jackson, *The Haunting of Hill House*

Not long ago, I met a young boy, around thirteen years old, who came to see me because his foster mother said he was *angry*. He was very tall, blond, and thin. He wore a bomber jacket, jeans, and yellow Crocs. The boy explained that his parents had hospitalized him fifteen times, beginning when he was only two years old. The hospital psychiatrists deemed him ODD (oppositional defiant disorder), a behavior disorder. Children diagnosed with the condition are uncooperative, rebellious, and hostile toward peers, parents, teachers, and other authority figures.

At six years old, his parents abandoned him in the system, and he disappeared. The boy described his early life as *unpredictable*. He used many words you wouldn't expect to hear from someone his age.

"I'm theatrical, impulsive, and menacing."

"How do you know these words?"

"The doctors and staff talk like that."

"What other kinds of words do you hear?"

"I'm uncooperative, detached, and unscrupulous."

"Unscrupulous?"

"Yes, I lack moral standards. I Googled it."

"Yes, I know what it means."

His foster caregiver, a kind woman with no experience nurturing children, told me she was afraid of him. "He just goes off," she said, "He shouts, and he even hits me."

The boy had spent most of his childhood in and out of what he called *facilities*, primarily children's jails, where they provide *treatment*. The treatment often consists of a psychiatrist prescribing antipsychotic medications under the diagnosis, housing, feeding, and maintaining order, never involving, or expecting the parents or caregivers to participate.

"Where were your parents?"

"They deployed to Milwaukee."

"Did they visit or call?"

"Not to my knowledge."

"You're 13. How do you talk like that?"

"Can we continue? Lunch is served promptly at noon."

The boy described when a guard from the hospital engaged him and other children in digging a waist-high hole with a spoon. When they finished, they filled in the gap with their hands. "We were learning cooperation and collaboration," the boy said. "Everyone participated in the activity," he added, showing a rare smile and a pensive giggle. "We chose the shortest kid to measure the hole." The staff sat on a picnic bench and smoked cigarettes.

While describing the events of that day, the boy reached into his pants pocket and pulled out a pink lighter. As I watched, he flicked the lighter twice, suddenly producing a flame. He held the lighter at arm's length and stared at it, seemingly entering a dream state.

I was curious.

He sat, the flame seemingly holding his gaze. Just as quickly as he had engaged the event, it was over. He blew on the end of the lighter as if preparing to taste something hot, cooling it, and then placed the lighter back in his pocket. "Where were we," he said, inhaling deeply and exhaling slowly.

"I don't get it," I said, adjusting myself in my seat and leaning forward.

"One of the guards left her cigarette lighter on the table, and I appropriated it," he said.

"Appropriated?"

"I swiped it."

"Thank you. Yes, I know."

"Are you going to tell on me?"

"I don't know," I said, "Why did you do that?"

"It makes me calm."

Mindful awareness, or being attentive to our mind where it is in the present moment, is believed to enhance our emotional state and is integral to emotional intelligence improvement.

We have only three options for focusing our thoughts at any given time. We either imagine the future, reimagine the past, or, more rarely, engage with the present moment. Imagining a terrible future filled with unmanageable outcomes creates anticipatory anxiety. Reimaging the past, reliving it instead of revisiting it, creates a mental state of depressive anxiety. Knowing where one's thoughts are, making judgments, and taking active steps to direct and redirect them, are often more possible when we engage in life in the present moment—without Fear of our imagination of what will happen to influence our choices.

The boy came to my office for several weeks. After getting comfortable with one another, his caregiver declared that the state had decided to *deploy* him to another state. His parents had decided they wanted him again.

"When are you leaving?"

"Maybe a month," he mumbled.

"Are you excited about finally getting a room of your own?" I asked.

He lowered his head. He pulled his hood so far over his face; it was tough to see his face, only the outline of his glasses and a small portion of his nose.

"I can't see you," I said, "I'd like to see your face."

He raised his head and pushed his hood back only slightly. "I don't like my face," he said, reaching up and lowering his hood over his glasses, leaving only his mouth showing.

"How do you suppose digging that hole helped you with your behavior choices?" I asked.

"It gave me something to do."

He paused and admired the candle burning on the wide coffee table in front of him. "I'm glad I got a chance to do something." He said, staring at the candle flame, again mesmerized.

EI theory endorses the belief that being in the present moment is the most optimal frame of reference for living peacefully. Being mindful of the present moment has shown to be a challenging mindset to sustain. Our minds are restless and constantly search for stories, memories, and imaginative ideas to entertain an otherwise uninspiring recognition of our dull moment. Mindfulness helps by focusing on the uneventful present and makes our thoughts less likely to engage the past or the future.

The boy arrived one day in a slump.

He could barely stay awake for our meeting. He explained that he planned not to swallow his medication and would throw it in the toilet without his caregiver's knowledge. "I'm always tired when I take those things," he complained. "I can barely stay awake to do my schoolwork," he sighed, "And then I get yelled at because I don't have any energy."

The COVID—19 pandemic forced most children to use technology for daily school instruction, making the process less socially engaging and susceptible, even without antipsychotic medication, to put children to sleep. "I can't stay awake," he said, yawning. "Then I go to sleep and can't sleep at night. So, I stay awake until it's time to get up."

The boy had started to gain weight and was concerned that his clothes were starting to fit too tightly. "I want to do my schoolwork and sleep normally, and I just can't do it with these drugs in my system." He lowered his head behind his hoodie. "I'm tired of getting yelled at."

Self-regulation often includes taking personal responsibility for both thought and behavior and being fair-minded in our judgments of ourselves and others. Although people who seek better-quality emotional intelligence begin their journey with heightened self-awareness, self-regulation will likely follow. Still, it will require a great deal more strategizing and effort.

Improved self-regulation in thought and behavior is a fundamental factor in any goal for emotional growth. Inter- and intrapersonal dynamic management, from an EI perspective, is aligned with the skill to manage thought and its consequent emotional expression. Building self-control is a goal in EI improvement.

Our goal is not to be emotionally isolated or unfeeling.

Quite the opposite.

Developing a more helpful form of self-regulation includes expanding the concepts of self-and-other acceptance, fair-minded judgment, appreciating the limits of human perfection in oneself and others, and recognizing the likelihood of human fallibility. Managing our disposition to regard anything short of perfection as unacceptable can be replaced with mindful acceptance—living the moment of life without comparison, bringing a quality of peace impossible through emotional distancing and disaffection.

The boy talked about being sent back to the hospital when his parents got bored or couldn't manage his sicknesses. He kept his head down as he explained that he had just gotten used to deploying. "They do it all the time in the army," he said. "And they come back like heroes. That's how I picture it in my head. Every time I deploy and come back, I'm a hero." He looked wide-eyed, "But it isn't easy to think that!"

Humans often think, emote, and behave gullibly, credulously, and superstitiously. Mindful acceptance may be one method for welcoming us into the potential of the present moment, where we can judge people, situations, and circumstances as they are rather than from some imagined perspective of what they should be.

The practice of mindful acceptance doesn't mean we will like everything we encounter or that we must give up and resign ourselves to what we face. Resignation and quitting are options; they are not the only options when choosing mindful acceptance.

We must accept the circumstance, issue, or idea before rationally engaging in change, improvement, or adjustment. Otherwise, we will not be engaging in solving the problem, only our imagination of the problem.

For example, we may wish to lose 50 pounds, but imagine that doing so will make us attractive, a success, and the valued human being we've always hoped to be. If we're not already enough as we are, we cannot expect to lose a single pound. If you begin any journey believing you are not enough already, you will start with a self-defeating mindset and will not likely reach your goal. If you think you are not good enough before starting your journey, you cannot expect to finish it.

Mindful acceptance means that we accept everything and everyone as they are, to whatever degree or form, the amount and measure they are with the moment. Conscious acceptance implies that our thoughts focus on the present moment and what it contains rather than what it does not hold. Mindful acceptance endorses the idea that we can, within the moment, handle everything about the moment if we stay with the moment. It may be true that we Fear being weak, so we imagine ways to avoid that possibility. However, the fact is that once we accept that we may not be as strong as we imagine ourselves to be, we can begin to strengthen ourselves. Strength is, after all, only possible after a period of sustained weakness.

The boy and I were nearing the end of our time together, after which he would be whisked away to another place, compelled to add unexpected layers to his budding identity, unfolding in some unpredictable way into adulthood. "Your mom and dad seem to care," I said. "I guess they can only do what they can do."

"My mum doesn't care about me," he said. "She wants everyone to feel sorry for her, so they won't think she's a bad mom."

"She's doing her best," I said softly.

"That's what my mum always said," he quickly responded. "She said it when I go back and when she's sending me away." Reaching into his pocket, he pulled out a blue mini flashlight. He pushed a button at the bottom, turned the light, and stared into the glow. He lost himself in it. I watched, trying to imagine what it could be he was doing.

"What is that you have there?" I asked, "Is that a flashlight? Wow, I didn't know they made them that small."

"Yes," he said, not taking his eyes off the light. "The lady took my Bic."

I watched his eyes focusing on light, seemingly captivated. "Can you tell me what you're doing?"

"I'm mesmerizing myself," he said. "It's how I calm myself and can make myself calm, and it just helps me stay focused and stop thinking about everything all at once."

I observed him for a few moments, not wishing to interrupt his grip on serenity. He seemed adrift in some space away from the therapy room, somewhere without uncertainty, insecurity, and doubt. He was, it seemed, centered and safe, and he wasn't afraid.

I recalled the trance-like relaxing effects of a campfire and how it was difficult to break my gaze. I have since learned that an open fire reduces blood pressure. The longer people sit in front of a roaring fire, the greater the relaxing effect. As it turns out, listening to fire crackling reduces blood pressure.

"I get it," I said.

"I knew you would," he said, staring again at his flashlight. "I discovered it, and it helps me get through my deployments."

"Can you describe how you feel?"

The boy said, "I am not a bad person. I am just me, and I don't have to be anyone else." He kept his eyes on the light as he spoke as if accessing some thought he was having at the very moment instead of recalling it from another time. "I don't need my mother to decide that about myself."

The light-gazing technique he used was something he had been practicing in private for a while. It seemed to hone his concentration and bring his mind to stillness. "What are you thinking about," I asked as I watched him focus intently on the light. Distractions seemed to dissolve away as his mind, and the light from the tiny flashlight came together. "What are you thinking about?"

"Just the light," he said, "I'm just thinking of the light." He let his thumb move to the switch at the bottom and returned it to his pocket. His face was visible for the first time in almost an hour.

"You seem o.k. now," I said, "What's this all about?"

"I just get a little break, and I can handle things," he said. "I talk inside my head a little better. It doesn't last, but I know what to do when I get like that." He turned on and off his flashlight, playing like a child. "I have to keep it secret," he added. "They always want to take my light away."

It is not uncommon for people to view EI theory to achieve emotional neutrality. That interpretation, unto itself, may reveal an opportunity for improved emotional intelligence.

We do not intend to render an individual emotionless, and emotional intelligence cannot be confused with seeking emotional perfection. The full array of our expressive potential is always at our disposal.

Regardless of how much gain we may have in our quest for emotional management, we are forever human and will likely continue to make mistakes in managing our lives and the emotion we use to express our thoughts.

It can take a lot of work to achieve this outcome.

No one ever drowned in sweat.

20

If It Doesn't Add to Your Life— It Doesn't Belong In Your Life

I think the future of psychotherapy and psychology is in the school system. We need to teach every child how to disturb themselves rarely seriously and how to overcome disturbance when it occurs.

—Albert Ellis

"We have trouble communicating. We argue about arguing, and we want to communicate better," said one member of the couple while the other sat and nodded in agreement. "Communication is our main problem."

"Can you describe the word communication?" I say, "What exactly do you believe needs improvement?"

"We disagree about everything," one said while the other demurred. "We shout and slam things."

"Do you expect a relationship that doesn't include disagreement?"

"Hmph," grunts one.

"See what I mean!" the other growls. "You have to help us! I can't stand it anymore."

"What would you like to do instead?"

"I'd like just to get along."

"What prevents that?"

"Communication," one said, facing the other. "We need skills, better ways of talking to each other!"

I pause and examine before saying, "Communication doesn't begin with speaking. It begins with thinking. If we can learn to think more rationally, we may improve the way we talk to each other," so sayeth the muse of emotional intelligence theory. I looked at them as they realized this wasn't their expected response.

There may be hundreds of theories of emotion, origin, and purpose in human life. EI identifies emotion as the language of thought, buffered against memory and often reinforced with elemental behavior. Using that definition, it appears, makes us not so different from goldfish. Beyond that idea, however, the purposeful use of emotion in human life is anyone's guess.

Emotion may have an adaptive function. We may slightly alter its appearance as each new generation replaces the last, purposefully helping to avoid the appearance of Fear with an artfully designed expression of strength. Emotion may be a false, exhausting approach that can quickly descend into depression, an emotional depth that words can never truly reach.

It could be that emotion as an actual, describable thing is an ongoing process, destined to never arrive at a finish line. Emotion may be a free-for-all, only to be interpreted by poets and deep thinkers. We can only hope to endure as a human race as we come to temporary conclusions about the meaning of emotion.

For example, the COVID-19 virus, the central theme of American life at this writing, stimulated our innate drive to endure, producing noticeable emotional adjustment in our individual and cultural connection with others.

The virus progressed through its fourth and fifth months of 2020, and sprigs of adaptation began to appear, revealing how we adjusted to the disease. These signs of endurance heralded our species' determination to prosper, even amid a worldwide pandemic, infecting and killing many people.

Our adaptation began with revising old ideas, concepts we weren't willing to easily forfeit, replacing them with more practical, life-sustaining methods for living.

With each determined effort, the force of modification on our algorithm for human emotional survival took on new, unexpected factors. We slowly noticed new growth, the influence of the will to live, eventually forming the branches we would use to engage in daily life.

Adaptation is an organism's physical or behavioral characteristic that helps it survive better in an environment. As we encountered and endured the virus, a newer form of mental health care emerged, making counseling more possible for those who could not, would not, or chose not to appear in person for a traditional therapy encounter.

"This is all new for me," I said to my new patient, holding a cell phone with a weaker-than-expected signal. The face-to-face software I started to use was not cooperating, leaving me to improvise our contact. "I think we can do this over the phone."

"I'm hoping we can," the woman said. "Everything is just a blistering mess. My husband is physically ill, and he's probably going to die. He is on a heart monitor, and they sent him home until this virus gets under control. He can't do anything and is in a terrible depression."

I looked at my cell phone as if it would provide information about the woman—something I could use to add a human dimension to her frantic, desperate voice. "I wish we could be in the same room," I said apologetically. "I think this thing we're doing works better when I see the whole person. I seem to be at an unexpected disadvantage."

The woman on the telephone continued. "I can't even go to the grocery store," she said frantically, "All these people running around wearing masks. I can't see their faces and don't know what they think. It's just terrible, and I'm scared to death!"

She seemed unaffected by my concerns about helping by telephone. She was glad to have someone to talk to about how afraid she had become.

"Can I ask you some questions?" I hesitated.

"The virus will contaminate the food if I go out and bring it home, and it will kill my husband," the woman said hysterically.

As I was unaccustomed to help by telephone, the sound of tears was a new language for me.

Or was that a sniffle?

Maybe she had allergies.

Should I ask if she's crying?

"Sounds like a real problem," I managed to say.

"I wear a mask and can't breathe," the woman continued. "I'm always out of breath. I run in and get what we need, and then I run out. I don't know this world anymore."

At this point in my discussion with a patient, one who was in person, I would attempt to explain anticipatory anxiety (the expression of Fear over anticipated events) by grabbing my brain model and pointing at the limbic system. I would describe the limbic system and how thought stimulates various brain areas. I would attempt to join her psychology with her anatomy to provide insight. As it was, we were on the telephone, and I was facing a distinct hardship.

As I listened to the woman on the phone describe the perils of living in a world under siege, I imagined how her brain was engaging its limbic areas and fueling her F^3 networks. "I wait in line to check out," she sighed, "and I try not to breathe."

The woman used the part of her brain that can only activate when we Fear what we believe will happen next. The F^3 system, the stress response, relies on the imagination of the future to activate the stress hormones necessary to fuel the fight-flight-freeze response. I asked, "What are you afraid of?"

There was a pause on the line.

I thought we had disconnected.

"I'm afraid of what will happen," I heard her say.

I waited, cautious not to seem dismissive. "What do you imagine is going to happen?" I asked, intentionally softening my tone.

"Terrible things," she whispered, "Very terrible things."

The woman seemed to overflow, detailing her thoughts as if the monsters she imagined were waiting for her over the horizon were actual and very much a threat. She described the coming catastrophes as if they were certain to happen. She imagined the very moment when her husband would lose his job and that he would immediately die. She imagined her death seconds later. "We've been married for fifty years," she explained. "I couldn't possibly live without my husband. It's just not possible."

Before dying a sudden, lonely death, she described how she would simultaneously lose her home and her familiar way of life. "I wouldn't be able to live anymore. He is my life, and we would both die and disappear. It's a terrible thought."

Our brains can draw on the past's details to manage the present moment, whether real or imagined, and use that information to imagine the future and prepare our minds and bodies for the worst. The skill for retrospective and anticipatory thinking may have resulted from early humankind's increasing need to commit more information to memory for survival.

As I recalled the structures of the brain and their operations, I tried to apply them to the woman on the phone and the reason for her call. "What do you imagine is going to happen?" she suddenly asked, as if realizing I was, in fact, part of the conversation. "What's your prediction on all this COVID-19 mess?"

"I'm not sure," I said, feeling as if I should provide a more supernatural explanation of how the government managed the coronavirus along a predictable timeline and an expected outcome. "I'm fairly sure whatever happens, we will all handle it. I am certain you will handle everything you encounter in the future." I paused to let it sink in. "Is there any reason to believe you couldn't handle whatever comes next?"

"I don't think you understand me at all. I feel so alone in all this." She sighed, audibly shuddering, "I'm so isolated." The woman continued: "I haven't been out of this house, except for running around like a mad woman, for almost three months. No one comes by anymore. My children are afraid of killing their father with COVID. No one ever said anything about being afraid of killing me! I don't think anyone cares about me anymore."

"Can you call your family and talk over the phone? Can you Skype or Zoom or chat on Facebook?" I asked, hesitating.

"You just don't get it!" she said, almost as if suddenly angry, her limbic system in overdrive, afraid of something else. "Talking over the phone is not a substitute for talking in person! I want to see and touch my family. I want to see who I'm talking to! It does make a difference."

The woman on the phone began to speak about her contributions to life, her children's development, and her career choices. She praised herself for her skill at housekeeping but questioned her success in raising her children. "They're all huddled together at their houses. I get an email from them. Email! I must have done something wrong. They could drive by and wave, maybe."

The woman continued to describe the luckless life she had come to live and expected to continue to live into infinity. She emphasized her mistakes as if stitching together the past, like a crazy quilt, but only using the most dreadful experiences she could recall. She brought her thoughts together to form the story of her life. "My husband and I have never been able to relax," she said. "My poor husband has worked his life away and never got a break. I don't know how we ended up in this mess."

"Has anything gone right?" I asked. "It sounds like your past and future are one big pig pile."

"You're right," she said. "We've had some nice times. Nice friends. No one calls anymore, which means a lot about that assumption. I feel like I live in the Serengeti." She paused, "How's your family?" she asked with sudden excitement. "Can I ask you that? Are you allowed to talk about yourself?"

"We are fine," I said, "Hoping for a vaccine."

"Have you heard anything?"

"I would like to ask you a question," I said. "It's a question I'm almost certain you've never heard, so please take a moment to think about your answer."

The woman took a deep breath and seemed to be preparing for a quiz. "O.K., I'm ready."

"I want you to describe your problems; only I don't want you to use the past or the future to describe your problems."

I waited while the woman seemed to think about the question. "Can you repeat the question?"

"Describe what is happening in your life at this moment. Don't use the past or the future to describe what is happening now," I said. "Just describe the present moment."

"Can I phone a friend?" She asked jokingly.

"Well, that wouldn't work," I said, joking back. "You don't have any friends. Remember?" I laughed.

"I'm scared," she said. "I won't be able to handle all of this. It's bigger than me."

"To be scared, you must imagine the future," I said softly. "The future is full of furry and scaly monsters. Describe the moment you're in right now."

"When you put it that way, my husband is upstairs watching *Price Is Right*, and my cat is sleeping in the laundry basket. The heat is coming through the vent, and my toenails are ragged. My roast smells great."

"What about the monsters you imagine headed for your home?"

"If I didn't think about the past and the future, I wouldn't have any problems." She seemed uncertain. "I'm standing here in my hallway with the phone stuck to my ear," she added. "It's hard to say, but if I don't think about the past and I don't think about what could happen next, I wouldn't have any problems."

"Spend a moment with that thought."

"It's hard to keep in my head."

"You imagine dragons. It's called anticipatory anxiety," I said, imagining the woman's face and her sudden awareness of how she contributes to her anguish. "You imagine monsters where there are none. You engage with monsters in never-ending, imaginary battles, and when you slay one, two or more spring up in its place. There is never an end to imaginary monsters. Even when you believe you have defeated one, you will return to it to check its pulse to ensure it is defeated. Because it is an imaginary process, anything is possible. Monsters can suddenly come back to life, and the battle begins again." I waited before speaking. "*Revisiting* the past is how we recall how we handled things in our past. *Reliving* the past will only continue the battles you've already fought. The future is unknown. We can make flexible plans for the future, but we cannot predict it in as much detail as you describe. We must take the uncertainty of time into our predictions and believe that we will handle it regardless of what happens. What else can you logically do instead?"

"You have a nice way of explaining things," she said and went silent.

I thought for a moment. "Can I ask you another question?"

"Sure," she said, "the last question seems to be going in and out of my mind as we speak." She laughed. "My head is swirling!"

"Describe *yourself* without using the past or the future to describe yourself."

"I'm still afraid."

"What are you afraid of?" I asked.

"I'm afraid I'm weak."

"What if you are weak? Do you always have to be strong?"

She paused. "I think I'm getting it. I'm not sure I can give up my Fear right now."

"I don't want you to think I am dismissive," I said, "but your problems are primarily imaginative. You reimagine events from the past, and then you imagine dragons in the future. Those are your problems. You forget that the present moment is all you have and will ever have." I waited for some acknowledgment. I heard a sigh. "You will have to begin to accept what is real, at this moment, over what you imagine about the future," I said. "You certainly don't have to like what is happening at the moment or what has happened in the past, but you will manage it much better if you can learn to recognize that it is what it is and that you can, and you will handle everything to come."

"I guess I could encounter my dragons when they fly into my life. That's if my imagination gives them wings." She laughed slightly.

"How about this idea? How about not all dragons being big and fearsome? You can shrink them to the size of puppies and watch them in the backyard from your kitchen window. You invented them," I said, "You can do whatever you want with them."

When we imagine the future as a catastrophe, our brains recognize the thought as accurate rather than imaginary and engage the same F^3 response. If we imagine an event, our brains will engage in the event. Catastrophic anticipation of the future will stress the body and the mind. Whether a fond thought or something less entertaining, we relive the past, eventually leading to depression. The past cannot be relived and result in anything but sadness. Instead, we might endeavor to live with the moment and revisit the past when and as needed.

This woman on the phone, whose husband was upstairs watching *Price Is Right;* whose children were preparing their dinner; whose pot roast was simmering in the crockpot, missed most of it, fearing imaginary dragons and frothing monsters. The woman couldn't fathom leaving her house; the woman who imagined her life was coming to an abrupt end asked, "If I don't plan it, how can I prepare for it?"

"The future is unknown to any exact detail. You can flexibly plan, but it's a crapshoot beyond that." I paused. "If you are here tomorrow, I guarantee you will handle everything. Use that concept in your flexible planning for the future."

Soothsaying, palm reading, astrology, and even religion, in many ways, are designed to make predictions of the future, providing some level of solace and hope for those who believe in such things. In truth, the future is unknown to any specific degree. We can use statistics, odds, probability, and likelihood, but we cannot surmise certainty. The only thing we can know about the future is to handle it. "You will handle it," I said. "You've already handled everything in your life up until this moment. And even this moment, you are handling. What makes you think the future will be any different? You cannot handle something that isn't real and increases in size and dimension depending on the boundless limits of your imagination."

"Yes," she said, sounding more confident.

"You can always make flexible plans. Did you believe three weeks ago that you wouldn't handle what you're handing now?"

"It took me three days to get up the courage to call you," she said, "All that time wasted being afraid of my imagination." She paused.

"Your cells have a memory," I said. "You cannot unknow something, and you have to decide to learn something newer, something stronger than what you think you knew."

"That discussion, my friend, is for another day," she said, "I'm exhausted."

"Yes," I said, "maybe tomorrow."

Exhaustion is often a sign that improvement in emotional intelligence is occurring.

No one ever drowned in sweat.

21

Move the Finish Line

*Life is complicated, partly because of the real difficulties we must
overcome to survive and partly because of our innate desire to always
do better, overcome new challenges, and self-actualize. Happiness is
experienced primarily in striving towards a goal, not having attained
things because our nature always wants to go on to the next endeavor.*
—Albert Ellis, *The Art & Science of Rational Eating*

While the human brain matures and acts as a thermally
insulated chamber like a kiln, a type of oven that produces temperatures
high enough to harden, dry, and chemically alter clay, creating pottery,
tiles, bricks, and even objects of extreme beauty. While we enjoy the
finished quality of pottery, we can easily overlook the mystery of its
creation. We can appreciate psychological theory this way, a

meandering string of elegantly crafted beads of wisdom and half-baked ideas.

As an aggregate, psychological theory assumes that we shape our human emotional flora and fauna intricately, weaving it from the tangled paths we travel through life. That singular idea may be responsible for hundreds of assumptions about the purpose and point of human emotional expression and psychological theory and practice.

There are notions of psychology that propose that humans are inherently aggressive, cooperating only to serve the purpose of dominance over others. Accounts of our warlike behavior date back to the first written records of our history and appear from that context to be a universal characteristic of social groups. Although we can reasonably expect cooperation and collaboration from others in modern society, humans can quickly revert to their primitive nature, relying instead on aggression and hostility to claim status over one another. From that perspective, we can describe the human emotional experience as a battle between inhibiting our aggressive nature in favor of transient, fragile partnerships with others.

For me, this phenomenon unfolds most often when I meet with couples, married or otherwise. One of the main reasons people seek counseling is for help with intimate and close relationships. People tend to pursue this type of counseling only when relationships are in crisis. Some problems are minor, and some are larger, but all are important and deserve exploration.

Communication issues are the primary reason couples seek counseling with my office. Communication seems to be the foundation of all relationships that often erode first. Intimate companions believe improving communication will save it when cracks appear in their relationship.

EI teaches that communication does not begin with speaking. Communication starts with thinking. EI teaches couples to improve communication by emphasizing more rational thinking, likely enhancing spoken communication.

Of course, we all think before speaking, but the distance between our lips and thoughts is often minimal. EI proposes that we spend more time pondering our thoughts before exchanging them with others.

The most substantial influence on communication between intimates is observing how others resolve disagreements and then mimicking them—speaking lines as if from a script. EI helps couples make a conscious choice in communication style, not from what they know from their past but from how they think at the moment. When we think more consciously before we speak, carefully examining the words we choose and the evidence to support our claims, we improve the odds that our message will be more precise. An emotionally intelligent discussion about love between couples may unfurl this way:

"You don't love me!"

"I do love you."

"Why do you always make me feel like you don't love me?"

"I've told you I love you. What more can I do?"

"You can show it!"

"I do show it."

"I don't see it."

"I love you the way I love you. If I showed you love some other way, it wouldn't be authentic. It would be some version of me that pleases you. Which would you prefer?"

"I'm not sure anymore."

"Oh, and I don't make you feel. You do that with your thinking. I love you, so I will help you with your thoughts if you want."

"All you have to do is just change how you behave."

"That would be enabling to you and self-destructive to me."

Premarital counseling can help address and answer potential misunderstandings, clarify expectations, and improve the definitions of marriage each person holds but rarely discuss before making this extraordinary commitment for life. Marriages built on assumptions, an indefinite nod-nod, wink-wink way to communicate expectations, will encounter a great deal of misunderstanding.

Working definitions of marriage before, during, and potentially after the commitment are often undefined. One example is how individuals use the word *couple* and what we can expect from *marriage*. EI endorses the use of truth, fact, and science when discussing the concepts of a lifetime of togetherness:

What do these words mean to you?

How do you envision a marriage?

What are your expectations of me in this marriage?

What do you imagine is your role in our marriage?

How do you like to engage in disagreement?

EI supports the idea that individuality is never lost even in a partnership, union, or companionship—words without clarification can seem boxlike, confining, and restricting without adding a personal definition.

Agreeing to a union is not a forfeiture of individual identity, beliefs, interests, or which friends we select. EI recommends strengthening individuality in agreements for lifetime companionship will result in unconditional acceptance, openness, and honesty as time unfolds to reveal other dimensions of individual character and ambition.

Companions are inspired to ask questions, request change or improvement, and discuss with their partners matters close to their individual lives with openness, hope, and kindness.

EI expects that companions will be more likely to engage with one another proactively when they do so as partners on a shared journey. Couples are alerted to the difference between *needing* and *wanting* from their companion. A *need* is a must-have, while a *want* is something you'd like but do not have to have as a condition of living your life contentedly. Relationships constantly change, and it takes daily effort to maintain them. Every day is a matter of breaking the tape hand-in-hand and moving the finish line incrementally forward for the subsequent pursuit of unconditional self-and-other acceptance.

Using these principles will be more complex than speaking scripts and playing characters from your past to resolve relationship disagreements. We may learn to take a minute, take a breath, and slow down before we engage in discussions of anyone's character or behavior, particularly that of our life partner. Giving what you can and asking but never demanding from your partner can result in more reasonable discussions and produce tangible outcomes.

Relationships are more complex when we seek to recognize the individuality and freedom of choice we all possess. We often fall for the demands of those close to us for Fear of losing the relationship, even when doing so compromises our individuality, integrity, and freedom to live true to ourselves.

When we place the honest, most sincere aspects of ourselves aside to please someone else, we are left unhappy and resentful. Agreeing to something you do not agree with and is not authentic will result in passive-aggressiveness, sneaking, hiding, cheating, stealing, and other unpleasantries.

Of course, we can agree if our companion asks for a behavior change. But compromise is not the only answer to questions of personal transformation. Other responses can be *no, yes, and maybe. I'll get back to you; I was thinking of that; Can you help me? I don't think I can do it on my own.* These are all valid responses to change requests. The most important part of the process is to respond to requests for change with genuine answers. It's always about finding the right fit for you and what you are willing to do, if anything, to transform your character. EI provides the following diagram for helping to ensure lasting companionships:

1. I do not base my unconditional acceptance of you on what you've done in the past or what I imagine you will do. I accept you unconditionally *at this moment*, with faults, strengths, and everything in between. I will let you know if anything changes, and then we can discuss it.

2. I retain my perfect right to ask you to change, and I recognize that I have no right to get what I ask from you. At this step, honesty and clarity are the keys. Answer the request with the most faithful response you can provide. The person seeking an answer has a right to know whether they will continue to accept you unconditionally. Depending on the solution, the individual can decide that they are eager to continue to welcome you unconditionally or to move to Step 3.

3. (You do not have to *like* what you accept, yet you can continue your relationship with your partner based on unconditional acceptance.) *Note*: If your request is met with

something not delivered, you can revisit Step 2 many times. However, the answers to your requests rest with you at some point. Here you would rely on your judgment of what you are getting against what was agreed.

4. If you cannot accept your companion unconditionally, you cannot have the kind of relationship you hope to have. When unconditional acceptance is not present, Love cannot be present. You have something other than Love. Your connection is likely a result of Fear, neediness, and delusion. You are encouraged to reassess your relationship from the perspective of unconditional acceptance and decide whether to dissolve it or move to Step 1.

Infidelity can be the most challenging conflict in maintaining unconditional acceptance. EI counseling can help find practical and meaningful ways to reestablish unconditional acceptance or dissolve a relationship amicably after these events. In cases where a couple has experienced infidelity, there are many options for managing it.

"You cheated on me! How am I going to forget the past and accept you unconditionally?"

"I'm sorry. I hope I won't do it again."

"How do I know that?"

"It's all I can offer."

"I can't live like that!"

These steps in improving communication may seem mechanical and out of touch with how people often behave in these or similar circumstances. (The truth is you already use these options with friends, co-workers, and strangers.)

Keep mindful that the steps are clearly defined. We expect you to use these suggestions by adding your personality, character, and flare. Individuality, your right to ask but not to get, and your commitment to unconditional acceptance are, regardless, the mainstays of the paradigm.

All relationships are complex, and there will be disagreement and conflict. EI relationship counseling can help couples grow individually while in a partnership. Emotional intelligence theory offers lessons for behavior change and the hope that we can engage with others in a way that recognizes the uniqueness of each individual in a relationship, free of Fear, neediness, and desperation.

One of the more intriguing encounters I had with a couple was when the George Floyd protests raged outside my office window, and COVID-19 was still in the air. I introduced myself to a young couple searching for help with *communication*. While protesters clashed with law enforcement, teargas exploded and ripped at the eyes of both nonviolent and anarchistic demonstrators; my clients made themselves comfortable, readying to discuss strategies for building intimacy and understanding with one another.

I had no guide for knowing the rules of engagement for pandemics or national protests, but the idea of love and companionship in this environment when it seemed all was lost endured anyway. The country was so divided at the time; it would have been inconsiderate to assume my consumers' positions. I admired their endurance and willingness to set it aside in the name of Love.

I sat wondering if I should mention the death of George Floyd, which was only minutes ago, fearing the perception that I was insensitive or too forward, too presumptive of their race and what I believed to be their mindset. "How are you doing with all this rioting?

What is happening in the world?" I asked. I picked up my iPad, preparing for notetaking.

"I don't pay much attention to the media," the woman said, smiling, "Is something happening?"

The man looked at me, his face covered with a blue paper surgical mask. "We've been talking about it at work," he said, barely audible, "Not much information."

Because the murder of George Floyd was only recently, I explained what was happening as the last event I heard before coming into the room.

"No, I don't know anything about it," the woman added.

The couple sat across from one another, and I remained twelve feet away, adhering to the guidelines set out by the CDC for psychotherapeutic engagements during the pandemic.

The woman explained that she and her husband could not express their thoughts to one another. "We have communication issues." She diagnosed her husband with *emotional fatigue*. "He may be a little narcissistic, too." The man added, from behind his mask, "She's always bugging me about stuff that isn't true. I don't cheat."

As we spoke, *trust* was a significant concern for her. "We need trust," the woman said, removing her mask and placing it in her purse. "We have no trust at all."

"We got to trust," the man said, his face remaining covered, only his eyes remaining visible, like an alligator peering over the waterline.

"We've been married twelve years. I think it's time we discussed trust," the woman added. "I think it's high time to discuss what a marriage is. Yes, let's have that discussion." She snapped the clasp on her purse shut. "I have been too strong for too long."

The man took the top from his water bottle, pulled down his mask, and sipped. "Let's do it," he said, placing the bottle between his leg and the chair.

"OK, let's talk about that time you had that woman . . . you had that person in the house," she said matter-of-factly. "Let's start with that and get it out of the way." She pursed her lips. She scratched her head with her pointer finger, looking at the ceiling, waiting for an answer.

"I told you she was a coworker," the man said, reaching again for his water bottle. "We used to work together, and she was just checking in on me."

"Who was the other one?" The man sat peering from behind his mask, saying nothing. "No trust. None. It's done," the woman said. "Everything flushed down the toilet." She moved her hand as if flushing a toilet. "Wooosh."

They sat staring at each other.

I took advantage of the pause. "How do you define *trust*," I asked. "What are your thoughts on trust?"

"I need to give you some background," the woman said. "There's a lot of background to this." She readied herself for a long, detailed story. I looked at the clock and noticed we had only 40 minutes remaining. "Can we go with the thoughts you have at the moment?" I suggested. "Without going into too much explanation. What do you mean by trust? In this moment, how would you define it?"

"What do we mean by trust?" she said, looking directly at her husband. The man shrugged and remained silent.

Although abstractions represent the fundamental building blocks of our associations with others, left unexamined, words like *trust, love,* and *anger* can conceal deeper meaning.

"We have to have a definition of trust if we demand it from one another, don't you agree?" I asked, making sure I made eye contact with both of them.

"Everyone knows what trust means," the woman said, "Right?" She glared at her husband.

Couples often use concepts and vague phrases to describe their feelings and expectations of one another. Ambiguity can lead to doubt without knowing how an individual defines words and ideas. Emotional intelligence theory encourages practitioners to construct a more exact definition of the terms and phrases couples use to describe their thoughts and feelings, especially idioms, metaphors, and figures of speech that can cause confusion and misunderstanding when left to individual interpretation.

"What does trust mean to you?" I asked the woman, placing the blunt end of my iPad pointer against my cheek.

When closely examined, I knew that trust could be a carefully disguised word for gaining a *guarantee* of future behavior. Trust is an *unconditional warranty* that what I say will never be altered. From the moment of the promise, trust is only moments away from being lost.

No one can guarantee their behavior over a lifetime. So confidence is not something we can ever expect from anyone, except when the promise of trust includes the guarantee of human fallibility. We may, instead of trust, offer *hope*, an assurance more likely fulfilled. We can promise *acceptance*. We may replace a guarantee of behavior with this oath: *Our relationship may change over time, but I will continue to have hope, and I will accept you, regardless of how you choose to behave. I may decide to do this from a distance, but I can promise those qualities will remain.*

I waited for the woman to add dimension to her vague demand for trust. "I don't understand the question," she said, drawing back as if a rubber bullet had buzzed past her ear.

"Trust," I said, "What do you mean by trust?"

"You know what I mean," she said. She looked at her husband. "I got trust issues because some people have lying issues."

The man raised his hands as if surrendering defeat. "I got nothin'," he said, lowing his arms back to his side and fitting the mask against his nose and chin. "This was your idea."

"What are you asking your husband to do?"

"I need something from him . . ." She paused. "I need to know if I should stay in this marriage," she responded, looking directly through me as if dazed and then back at her husband, "I don't think it's too much to ask. Do you?"

Rational couples counseling does not endorse concepts and meme-ish phrases to define an integral part of an intimate relationship. Sensible couples counseling envisions facts and evidence are more valuable than abstract words and phrases to describe the link between mates.

"How is this loss of trust a problem for you?" I asked.

"It's a problem because he does whatever he wants, and I'm not going to have it anymore."

"What are we trying to achieve today?" I asked, "What are you afraid of at this moment?" I asked. "Can we examine your thoughts?"

Couples who seek improved emotional intelligence are frequently asked to take a perspective or reveal a mindset that may seem counterintuitive. Couples are invited to abandon the idea that being *one person* is not a reasonable goal of EI counseling.

Relinquishing individuality as a condition of forming a partnership is antithetical. There is not and can never be one person made from two unique individuals, making this goal unachievable. Likewise, personal motivations, drives, and privacy are not forfeited to form a healthy relationship. On the contrary, these qualities are celebrated as the elements of our character that should attract us to one another.

Individuality is a fundamental measure of human life and cannot be plausibly compromised without severe consequences to the partnership. Establishing developmental independence is an inherent drive within us, a system of building and maintaining a sense of self, made possible through self-reflection and the expression of self-confidence.

The establishment of individuality makes encountering others more possible after meeting our personal needs, goals, and desires. Entwining such a delicate, fundamental human growth system with that of someone else in such a way as to make the process unrecognizable for either person can fundamentally weaken any relationship.

Intimate partnerships must recognize that such a convergent journey must expect and meet modification, adjustment, and variation with optimism. We must consider the relationship's potential to end with time if we neglect to understand that the partner is an individual.

Codependence or the excessive reliance on others for a sense of identity can look and feel like what we believe is a sign of love. Codependent relationships signify a degree of unhealthy clinginess and neediness where one or both persons do not have self-sufficiency or autonomy and rely on the other for individual fulfillment. Phrases like *I am nothing without you; you complete me; or you are my better half* could be construed as signs of unhealthy companionship, a character that two people who are not whole in their own right have encountered one another to engage in a healthy partnership. One is entangling the other for a lifetime leading to suffocation.

We must first be complete in our own right. The price to pay for individuality cannot be too high for the privilege of knowing yourself. Healthy relationships demand healthy individuals, self-sustained individuals, and fully actualized on their own terms. Of course, individuality is an ongoing process. Still, intimate partners must be willing to recognize when the relationship takes on an unhealthy identity and that ending the partnership is the best decision for one or both.

The converse of this idea is the familiar demand for *compromise*. This approach negates the powerful influence free will has on decision-making and, like all decisions to change one's behavior, must be chosen willingly. When faced with making other, less oppositional choices, we can expect complications. Compromising over the authentic self can lead to deception, adding different, less flattering dimensions to our character. An honest answer to a request to change is vital. We must not agree to behavior change that we are not genuinely willing or capable of delivering.

"Will you stop smoking for me?"

When we meet a request to change from the perspective of maintaining stability in the relationship rather than genuinely choosing to change, we may say, "Yes, honey, I love you. My smoking is over for good! Just let me finish this one." Eventually, the truth and broken promise will appear, left like a stamped-out cigarette butt in the gutter. "I found your cigarettes in the basement behind the water heater."

"Oops."

"What else are you lying about?"

The enduring issue in couples counseling appears to be that one or both individuals believe they should, must, have to, and need to get the change they seek from their partner as a condition of continuing the relationship. Rational couples counseling includes the idea that individuals never surrender their perfect right to ask their partner to change. We must remember that we never have a right to get what we ask, making unconditional acceptance much more difficult.

The paired living potential is more likely to continue if we encounter honesty, positive self-regard, and authenticity. When we offer honesty instead of deception, we replace obedience with individualism.

Mistrust, lying, sneaking, and duplicity are often the result of false promises for change, culminating over time in one partner asking the other, "I knew you wouldn't do it when you promised! Why do I keep trying with you?" Often leading to a relationship built on doubt, suspicion, and caution—fear. We may, instead, discuss behavior change this way:

"Will you stop smoking?'

"No, I'm not ready to make that promise."

"If you love me, you'll quit."

"That isn't true. I'm not willing to lie to you to prove I love you."

After thirty minutes, the couple sitting in my office could not attempt to define the concept of trust. While the woman became visibly uncomfortable, her masked husband seemed uninterested. She turned to face me. "I thought we would be talking about the *Five Love Languages*," she said, "I disagree with your approach, and I like the *Five Love Languages* better."

"Did you happen to read my website before you came in?"

"We don't read websites," the man said, crossing his arms over his chest.

"I wanted to talk about the love languages. Have you read the book? You must have. You're a therapist, and everyone's reading it."

"Should I stay while you discuss these ideas of love languages?" I asked, perplexed, "I practice emotional intelligence improvement." I looked them in the eye. "That's all I do. It's my schtick. I help people improve their emotional intelligence."

"We don't know what that is."

"What are you afraid of when your husband behaves as he does?" I asked.

The woman shifted in her chair, dismissing my statement and continuing with her description of her relationship with her husband—if only he would cooperate and learn her love language. "I disagree with you," she said, "I'm not afraid—I'm pissed."

"If we engaged that idea that you're pissed, what do you think about when you think your husband is visiting with unfamiliar women in your home while you're at work?"

The woman looked at me and back at her husband, holding her breath. "Stop it!" she suddenly shouted. "I'm not here to talk about being afraid. I'm trying to fix this marriage. Just STOP IT!"

"What are you willing to do to fix your marriage?" I asked. I watched as the man's eyes darted from her to me, the rest of his face concealed behind his crinkled paper mask.

"He can already trust me," she said, seemingly giving up, "I can't trust him."

"What do you imagine he can do to help you trust him?"

She paused before suddenly saying, "He can stop cheating."

"He told you he doesn't cheat."

"He is cheating," she said, "Anyone can see that."

"If he is cheating, how is that a problem for you?" I asked, "What would it mean about you if he cheated?"

"About ME?"

My eyes went to the clock. The extra fifteen minutes I had spent listening to stories of the past and imaginations of the future. "I don't think your problems relate to your husband's behavior. I think you imagine what your husband's behavior means *about you* now and what it means about your future. That is where you can find your Fear." She stared at her tissue. "If your husband is cheating and you choose life without him, what makes that a problem for you?" I continued, "What if the worst thing that could happen did happen?"

She sat for what seemed like years. "I'm afraid I will be alone," she finally said. "I'm afraid I will be alone for the rest of my life. I'm afraid I will be a failure. I'm afraid I'm not good enough. I'm afraid I did something wrong." She sat quietly for a moment, thinking. "I think I just had a near-death experience," she finally said, "Are you happy now?"

"Good job," I said, "That's the Fear we're looking to find. You found it!"

The masked man became fidgety.

"I guess we are out of time. I hope to see you back next week."

As the couple left my office, I hoped they would eventually discuss Fear, loneliness, and empirically-based decision-making. In my mind, I heard an argument for the *Five Love Languages* instead.

At the same time, the firestorm raged as hundreds of people across the country marched the streets, demanding to be heard, most of whom witnessed the murder of George Floyd at the hands of the Minneapolis police.

News of the pejorative activities of some to undercut the temperament of the demonstrators filled the airways. Fear was being comingled with aggression, preventing people from staying on message. Confusion, uncertainty, and an overwhelming sense of urgency replaced the hidden message, "I am afraid! I'm afraid of my place in the world. I'm afraid for my children. I'm afraid I have no purpose beyond the stereotypes I symbolize to you. I'm afraid I have no options. There is no communication!"

People carried signs, sometimes wearing masks to prevent the spread of COVID-19. Some held their fists in the air, while others walked together to show strength and unity. Looting dominated the airways, obscuring the intended message, "I am afraid, and I cannot be heard when I shout my message."

Violence co-occurred with harmony, disguising the message even more, "I am afraid, and I don't know what else to do." The president had not yet met advocates calling for change, likely to blame his disinterest on the ambiguous message sent from the battlefield. Neither had he traveled to Minneapolis to speak with the community about George Floyd or listened to the Fear. No effort, it seems, was made, leaving the streets ablaze with Fearful people with no way to communicate other than with more Fear and violence.

Biology describes symbiosis as a close, prolonged association between two or more different organisms of different species that may, but does not necessarily, benefit each other. Because other species often inhabit the same spaces they share or compete for the same resources, they interact in various ways.

There are five basic types of symbiosis: mutualism, commensalism, predation, parasitism, and competition. An example of mutualism is the clownfish and how it benefits the sea anemone by consuming parasites. Parasitism is the interaction between two species where only one benefits from the other organism and harms the other. In parasitism, one organism benefits at the expense of the other by stealing resources. The clownfish feeds the sea anemone with nutrients from its excrements in mutualism. The parallels between human relationships and the definitions of symbiosis are ringing.

Many people feel the relationship between humans and their pets is symbiotic mutualism, where there is little judgment, replaced with unconditional positive regard. We may describe human relationships that provide reciprocal benefits as mutual symbiosis.

We may spend our lives trying to be in sync with others, being like them, rather than building mutual symbiosis by accepting differences and sharing strengths. Being alike cannot be the driving force in measuring the success or failure of our partnerships.

Living in symbiosis or having both independent and interdependent companionships, not only with an individual but with the broad spectrum of society, could be the thing we can use to improve emotional intelligence. You are always just one decision away from an entirely different life.

Relationships using EI theory as a foundation is a tough slog. No one ever drowned in sweat.

22

Mind Your Business

The emotionally mature individual should accept that we live in a world of probability and chance, where there is not, nor probably ever will be, any absolute certainties, and should realize that it is not at all horrible, indeed-such a probabilistic, uncertain world.

—Albert Ellis

Nothing is more valuable in EI improvement than mindful meditation. We can estimate the value of this mental relaxation technique in the amount of practice we put into it to make it something reflexive rather than an afterthought. Without yoga mats, incense, and soothing music, we can improve our present awareness using the opportunities we encounter in real life. We may use a chime coded to our phone to specific times of the day that reminds us to take two minutes to relax our brains. Using prompts can remind us that it's time to pause. No matter where we are, we can focus on our breath and only our breath for two minutes. If our plans are reasonable, we will get used to including the practice in our daily lives. Make mindful rest possible on a bus, sitting in a movie theatre, or doing our chores.

It is not uncommon for your mind to wander into the past or the future during mindful meditation. When that happens, notice it. Let the thoughts pass through your mind and be curious of the event.

I often imagine that my thoughts are a cluster of balloons floating overhead. I visualize these balloons in my thoughts: blue, red, yellow, black, and green. Sometimes I am tempted to reach up and grab one or more of them and pull them into me. Instead, I admire their unique colors, the sun shining on their rubbery surfaces, and the sound they make when they encounter one another. Sometimes I grab one or two of these balloons, the most disagreeable ones, and pull them into me. It's always easier to reach up and grab them. It is more difficult to release them back to where they belong. I hold them and feel the force of their energy. Images of the past and the future suddenly overwhelm me. I know my life depends on releasing them. I remind myself that the thought these balloons elicit is not me and that I can observe them without holding them or drawing them in.

I can be curious without Fear.

I release the balloons and return my mind to my breathing, feeling my chest fill with air and slowly empty, like giving the balloons the air they need to float away.

As you practice your mindful techniques, you will reach out and grab a balloon without knowing it and hold it—grip it tightly. There have been times when I have simultaneously grasped two or more of these balloons in my hands, careful not to lose them. I observe this peculiarity in myself and how I behave. I am not afraid of my thoughts or memories. At some point, I let them return to their flock.

I observe them.

I watch the colors mix and mingle with the others, observing as my mind returns to breathing.

If you choose this method of mindful rest, notice your thoughts and be curious about them. Let your thoughts enter and leave, like floating balloons, no longer trapped in a cycle of Fear.

Return to your breathing and observe it.

Notice how your chest rises and falls. Hear your breath entering through your nose and mouth into your lungs.

Listen as you expel the air.

What can you learn from being present?

Our human wiring is to avoid pain and to seek pleasure. Our recollection of the past and our imagination of the future are seemingly great places to draw information, believing that in doing so, we can reduce or even eliminate the insurmountable challenges we imagine to our goals.

We link our thinking about how well we will manage distress, discomfort, and despair. We immediately imagine the results as overwhelming when we focus on what could go wrong or what has gone wrong. Our imagination often results in a downward spiral into a state of absolute urgency to know the outcome before establishing the facts.

Emotional intelligence improvement does not endorse negative or positive thinking in managing emotional well-being. They are each products of magical thought notions. EI practitioners use rational thought derived from truth, fact, and science to manage their minds and bodies.

Typically, rational thinkers perceive the situation for what it is and manage to find solutions to problems now. Of course, analytical thinkers prepare for the future but use flexible thinking. Solutions based on truth, fact, and science can influence the present situation when the imagination does predict a fixed outcome.

Worriers and those who chronically anticipate disaster, distress, and despair often experience a lower immune response than those who use a rational, solution-focused strategy. The poor immune response is in the approach, and the obstacle is typically the focus rather than the thinking that influences the difficulty's size, shape, and proportion.

"If she would stop talking to me that way, I'd be happy."

"How do you intend to stop her from talking that way?"

"I don't know, but she should stop!"

"How about managing your thinking about how she is talking?"

"How could that help?"

"It's not how she's talking. It's your perception of her talking. You can't change her, but you can change your thinking."

"I don't know how to do that."

"Let's begin with relaxing our minds and being curious of our thoughts."

When faced with an obstacle, we can manage using an emotion-focused strategy, emphasizing our troubled thinking and attempting to find a solution. However, the tricky part is we can't oversee a nutty head with a nutty head. We may find more opportunities if we manage our bodies first, from the toes up, relaxing our minds.

There is no precise way to cope with setbacks to our goals. EI improvement provides options that may produce better results. Emotion-focused coping may be more adaptive, but problem-focused coping may be better. In either case, however, managing the body first and its response to frightening thoughts is ultimately the first option using either strategy.

You may choose emotion-focused coping when there is nothing you can do about the obstruction. For example, when the impediment is a traffic jam or a failing grade. Managing the body and thinking can lead to better emotional outcomes. Problem-focused coping may wonder why the basement flooded and why the leak shouldn't be there. This strategy won't decrease the surge, and problem-focused coping approaches will not likely improve the result.

Of course, these conceptualizations of emotional growth will need to be explored, carved out, and made into valuable competencies that lead to practical skills. Emotional intelligence improvement, after all, is a lifelong endeavor, so we can expect to have enough time to reach whatever goals we set.

EI improvement hopes to make it to the top of your to-do list. For now, ponder the idea that the voice inside your head, your self-talk, cannot be you. You must become the one who hears it, the one who challenges it, and the one who must discover healthier options.

Emotional intelligence forms the juncture at which cognition and emotion meet; it facilitates our capacity for resilience, motivation, empathy, reasoning, stress management, communication, reading, and navigating many social situations and conflicts.

Bringing clarity and functionality to these definitions of emotional disturbance while including other converging ideas will serve as our springboard for improved emotional intelligence.

EI can lead to more adaptive ways of thinking, feeling, and living.

It takes work.

No one ever drowned in sweat.

23

It's Not the Goal—It's the Process

. . . every day, thousands of people appear before a jury of their peers and hope they will be judged fairly when they are judged by human brains that always perceive the world from a self-interested point of view. To believe otherwise is a fiction that is not supported by the architecture of the brain" —Lisa Feldman Barrett, *How Emotions Are Made: The Secret Life of the Brain*

Improved emotional intelligence encourages better-quality self-and-other awareness, self-regulation, self-talk, and mindfulness. Self-awareness is not to be confused with self-consciousness.

We can define *self-consciousness* as the perception of one's environment, body, and lifestyle compared to others; conversely, *self-awareness* detects one's mind, thoughts, motives, and desires without comparison or contrast. EI theory chooses self-awareness over self-consciousness.

Self-awareness may take two forms: *conceptual* and *embodied*. We can detect conceptual self-awareness in how we compare ourselves to others. This self-awareness relies on judging and evaluating ourselves and others using comparison, an abstract image of human perfection, leading to illogical conclusions:

I am good because I compare well to my neighbors. We dress alike, and we think alike. We have the same goals and ambitions, are always polite and friendly, and never disagree.

Embodied self-awareness, conversely, seeks to establish an inner state of self-evaluation, bringing attention to the sensory experience only available by being with oneself in the present moment.

I am neither good nor bad. I've established my customs, traditions, and behaviors around my preferences. I speak my mind when my mind talks to me. I am the arbitrator of how I live and what I believe. I accept that others are not like me. I do not seek to comply with an external standard for myself.

Embodied self-awareness inspires a less conceptual relationship with oneself and replaces it with more fact-based truth and authenticity. For example, we often compare our bodies to a narrow standard of beauty, leading to *self-consciousness*. Never satisfied and never measuring up, our bodies become our enemies, and our self-awareness becomes *conceptual*. We conclude, in effect, that we cannot live comfortably within ourselves unless we meet a social construct for beauty, rendering every event, experience, and thought an act of war against ourselves. We develop a self-abusive inner dialogue, corporal self-evaluation, and magical thinking to conclude that contentedness ends only with external approval.

Instead, we can use more fact-based internal language, more closely aligned with honest self-awareness, and less about the comparison: *embodied self-awareness*. In a state of the embodied self, we take in all we experience moment by moment, staying present with every sensation. From this perspective, our cells, organs, and tissues communicate and collaborate to produce an emotional state that external evaluation could never equal.

"I'm fat."

"Compared to who?"

"Everyone."

"How is that a problem for you?"

"I look terrible."

"How do you know that?"

"Take a look. You tell me."

"I see you."

"Then you know what I mean."

"What should I be seeing?"

"A big fat loser."

"I don't see that. That's what you see."

When our goal is to compare better, we create a mindset that deprives us of the inner peace that is only possible in the absence of contrast. Embodied self-awareness is living alongside others while detached from the self-destructive act of comparison. Instead, the self engages in objective self-discovery, producing a system of self-meaning built from provable facts, verifiable truth, and flexibility.

Comparison, by definition, is to render one thing more or less than something else. We may expect to use this judgment system for cars, bananas, and hats, but it's another thing to use this technique to judge or draw conclusions about ourselves and others. If a comparison is a mortar that binds our system of self-meaning, it will not sustain the magnitude of individual variation each of us possesses. Comparison encourages the individual to set aside the authentic self and replace it with something inauthentic, something we sustain with Fear of exposure, like the façade of a building or wall that cracks and falls away, revealing the materials beneath.

Many of us are driven daily by how well or not we exist compared to others. We commonly define a human error as an absolute failure, a sign of utter worthlessness by comparison. We often place an unnecessary amount of mental and physical energy into trying to hide our mistakes, relentlessly patching the cracks in our façade, hoping that it will stay put for another day.

The act of social comparison does not allow for the expression of an authentic, self-driven identity. Instead, we seek to be only the equivalence of conformity, making no room for individuality and difference.

Rather than seeking commonality and sameness with others, those who express embodied self-awareness avoid using labels, classifications, and narrow characterizations to describe themselves and others. Acknowledging oneself as a unique person can encourage self-acceptance and lead to more favorable, flexible, and less judgmental relationships with others.

Each of us possesses our own system for describing ourselves, producing what may be called *self-meaning*. Our thoughts are a historical match to what we have always told ourselves about the same things over our lifetime. We often influence self-meaning with imagination and magic. For instance, we may imagine that being richer would bring us the joy we guess is more abundant for others wealthier than ourselves. We may then construct a self-meaning that does not include the person at the moment but an imaginary facsimile of someone else. In that regard, we avoid the potential for joy in life; we live in favor of something constructed of imagination and magic that is much better than who we are, honestly.

EI theory endorses the idea that self-meaning is the act of doing without Fear of criticism, accepting imperfection, treating others fairly, and expecting the unexpected. We choose curiosity over Fear and are willing to explore new things, take risks, and learn through mistake-making.

We may be more emotionally intelligent by claiming our self-meaning without making our successes and failures, achievements, and flops the definition of who we are. Albert Ellis, the father of cognitive therapy systems, proposes twelve examples of how we can sabotage self-meaning:

1. We hold the idea that being loved is a dire necessity. Instead, we may concentrate on self-awareness and self-meaning, winning approval for practical purposes, and loving rather than being loved.

2. We believe that certain acts are awful or wicked and that people who perform such actions should be damned. We may think that certain acts are self-defeating or antisocial and that people who do these things misbehave. We could help if we accepted people's poor behaviors make them rotten individuals.

3. We believe situations and circumstances are horrible and demand they should not be. Instead of the idea that we can choose to change the things we don't like, we had better accept everything as it is first. (Acceptance of fact does not

imply that you will like what you get; it is simply a matter of receiving the facts as they exist.)

4. We believe that misery is caused by what happens to us, believing that it is forced on us by something out of our control. We can assume that our *view* of deplorable conditions causes our emotional state and that although a situation is not agreeable, we can permanently alter our perception of it.

5. We believe that if something is or may be unpleasant, dangerous, or unsafe, we should be upset and endlessly complain and obsess about it. Instead of the idea that we can face whatever obstacle we encounter and render it not dangerous by altering our perception. We can accept the inevitable if that is our only choice.

6. We may hold that it is easier to avoid than to face life's difficulties and responsibilities instead of thinking that the effortless way is usually a much more complex overall route.

7. We may believe that we need something other, more robust, or greater than ourselves to rely upon instead of the idea that it is better to hear our minds, accept risks and responsibilities, and act less dependently.

8. We may believe we should be thoroughly competent and intelligent and achieve every goal we set. Instead, we may cultivate the idea that we can do quite well with our imperfections and accept our human limitations and fallibilities.

9. We may hold that because something once strongly affected our life, it should affect it forever, instead of the idea that we can learn from our past experiences but not be overly attached to or prejudiced by them. The past only exists in your mind and does not represent the present moment.

10. Some of us may hold the idea that we must have control over things that affect us instead of the opinion that the world is full of improbability and chance and that we can still enjoy life despite this. We can encounter every obstacle, but only when it is in our way.

11. We may believe that we can achieve happiness through inertia and inaction instead of the idea that we tend to be happiest when we are vitally absorbed in creative pursuits or devote ourselves to people or projects outside ourselves.

12. We may believe that we have no control over our emotions and cannot help feeling disturbed. Instead, we may strengthen the statement that we have absolute control over our destructive thoughts if we change them.

Self-meaning is best when it is fair, patient, and empathic, and it is the framework for taking a more equitable perspective on how to live as humans among humans. Instead of a species seeking to perfect ourselves, we must recognize that we are a compilation of weaknesses, strengths, and average traits that are a complete mosaic of our lives.

Strength in self-meaning is a daily chore, requiring attention, devotion to the goal, and a willingness to fail.

No one ever drowned in sweat.

24

Three Things Only Two Guys Know

A person will be just about as happy as they make up their mind to be. —Abraham Lincoln

Magical thinking is a common source of the causal inferences we draw without clear facts. Unlike the confusion of correlation with causation, magical thinking does not require the events to be verified. Magical thought forms all or part of our expressions of love, jealousy, depression, guilt, and anger and is the foundation for murder.

Most of us depend on figments of the imagination to manage our minds. Fantastic recollections of the past snuggly merged with the future to define the moment of our lives.

When we focus on the past or the future, we are not accepting our powerlessness over things we cannot control. We imagine or reimagine our lives through a veil of illusions, unwilling to accept the past, confident that the future holds an equal measure of misery. We replace our reality with our imagination. We destroy our relationships, Fear risk, and reject opportunity from this perspective. We all do this to some extent as we interpret the world and each other through our perceptual filters. While this practice is hazardous, EI improvement hopes to modify our time in this activity, emphasizing what is happening now and not slaying imaginary dragons in the future.

I once met a man who said, "I know three things only two guys know." He came to my office to make that statement and stayed only ten minutes. He held his finger up to his lips, said, "Shhhhhh," and stood to leave.

I was immediately interested.

I don't know why my curiosity peeked higher than anything anyone has ever said to me. My mind locked onto the idea that there was a secret, and I could not let go until it was revealed.

What did he know?

Could I get it out of him?

How could I be the third guy to know?

I asked, "Do you want to talk about it?" knowing that the door that hid his secrets needed a key. "Whatever it is, I won't judge you."

"I won't tell you," he said.

As a therapist, I view my role as the receiver of secrets—the holder of the hidden. Although I often listen to almost everything else with my thumb and forefinger on my chin, secrets are more alluring. The intentional concealment of thoughts is a challenge, and once the individual reveals the mystery, my job becomes more work than intriguing.

This man was different.

"Are you afraid to discuss your mind?" I asked, crossing my legs. "Revealing your mind is what motivates psychological improvement."

"It won't work," he said, sitting back down, "I won't tell you."

Telling a secret and receiving understanding from others is often freeing, much like penance after confessing sins to a priest. There are consequences for keeping secrets. Although we can compromise our physical and emotional health, pain avoidance or the burden of hiding secrets can motivate us to reveal them. Similarly, a secret may negatively impact the recipient of the intimate information.

The commitment to concealing secrets for someone else can be burdensome and cause inner conflict and distress. The inheritor of the secret may feel compelled to tell the secret to someone else—to unload it.

It may be true that we can never keep a secret forever, often the length of our promise to keep it. The cost of mental and physical health may outweigh the confidence of the commitment to keep it.

The average person keeps thirteen secrets, five of which they have never told another living soul. This statistic may explain why we seek physical and emotional healthcare.

It is not easy to keep secrets. But we believe we cannot have close relationships without sharing them. Most of us think that concealing information from others, especially intimate partners, interferes with intimacy, rendering the relationship inauthentic and dishonest. Making room in the *heart* for new, genuine experiences motivates sharing hidden thoughts, memories, and ideas.

Some of us avoid closeness altogether because of our secrets. We think we cannot meet the authenticity mark for true intimacy, so we take relationships only to a point. Some may attempt intimacy but find that their reluctance to share secrets defines the term of a relationship.

People who hide their secrets think about them twice as often as those who choose not to conceal them. The more our minds wander toward a mystery, the more we damage our well-being and sense of connectedness with others.

"Keeping secrets makes me mysterious," the man said. He took a sip from his water bottle. "I feel like the redeemer and the sinner simultaneously, metering out judgment and showing no mercy." He paused and smiled. "I keep myself in hell that way."

"Would you feel better if you shared your thoughts?" I asked, "Wouldn't that be a better solution?"

"My secrets are tormenting," he said. "I bleed for them." His eyes welled with moisture, but no tears fell. "I'm only here to tell you I have secrets." He removed his COVID-19 facemask from his pocket and attached it to the back of his ears. "That's all I came to say." He stood to leave. "Thank you for your time."

"You've only been here a few minutes," I said, putting on my facemask and reaching for the doorknob.

"Yes," he said, "It only takes ten minutes." He passed me and opened the outer door. "I never stay longer than ten minutes."

"Why?"

"It intensifies my pain." He pointed his finger in my direction. "We can destroy lives in ten minutes."

"We can save lives in ten minutes."

"Yes, my point exactly."

Emotional expression is an intriguing communication system and manages dynamic input and output, often producing a confounding, unexpected result. When the message isn't clear, we want to know *Why.*

Humans are designed to discover what's behind the curtain. We are curious to a fault, never satisfied until we see everything concealed. We operate under the impression that to manage our lives we must thoroughly understand everything hidden that has touched our memories or will destroy our dreams.

Seemingly programmed to uncover, investigate, and reexamine every piece of our memory to provide answers to our present problems, we profoundly focus on analyzing the *Why* in everything. This purposeful effort significantly influences our emotional state when its persistence results in only more questions. We will cycle that question without a clear answer until we have one. Our minds cycle, sometimes for the entirety of our lives, leading to chronic states of despair as it becomes more apparent that no answers can satisfy that preoccupying desperation to know.

While questions of *Why* can benefit when answerable, our often vague and murky memories can lead to confusion and emotional instability. Trusting what we remember is the biggest hurdle because even that information source becomes suspect just minutes after an event. Yet we continue to avoid the value of the present moment instead of the vagueness of not knowing.

Life often unfolds unexpectedly, leaving many unanswerable questions in its wake. Still, for many, the solution to each mystery of the past is integral to managing the moment we occupy.

Why do I feel this way?

Why am I treated this way?

Why was I mistreated?

Why am I always the victim?

Humans use language primarily to talk to themselves and others about other people, find out who is doing what, succeeding, behaving heroically, or failing miserably.

Once, knowing the answers to every *Why* gave us a distinct advantage in human evolution. Our ancestors relied on the past for accurate data to plan what we would do to improve our survival later. We framed our past actions accurately, with as little imaginative input as possible, to establish a reliable source for safety, shelter, and food—information crucial to existing in the present moment. Before designing formal statistics, our predecessors imagined likelihood, probability, and odds and used the results as their guide.

Recalling our experiences, particularly with the weather, helped make survival more likely. Remembering where the buffalo roamed, where the dryest caves could be found or recollecting the life and death information found in the fetid odor of decay is no longer as important as it was once. Memory is now less practical and more of a self-sabotaging diversion from the present moment.

We often imagine being somewhere other than the moment we occupy. Likewise, we worry about handling everything to come instead of using data and reliable information found in the present moment to help resolve our emotional conflicts.

Once, our relatives climbed trees and watched for signs that climbing down was a risk. Now we sit in trees with no way to come down because our enemies are imaginative and, therefore, ever-present. Our minds create even more wolves when the one we imagined wanders away, monsters with sharper claws and even sharper teeth.

If we seek to know *Why* (this has happened to me), we seek answers to questions that have little relation to addressing the present issue and can only result in hopelessness. In contrast, questions of *How (can I manage my mind so that I can do something about this)* bring power and confidence to engage the present moment as it is and not what we imagine it to be.

EI theory is well-grounded in knowing what makes something work and sustains that idea. *Why* is not often the question seekers of improved emotional intelligence are prone to ask when problem-solving, whether it's an emotional or problem-focused issue. EI practitioners know that life frequently unfolds unexpectedly, so instead of asking *Why* we ask *How* and engage in systematic problem-solving from that perspective.

How am I making myself feel this way?

Knowing why we feel the way we do or why something happened provides little opportunity to engage with the present moment. Likewise, there is no skill in answering questions that have no potential for being proven, mainly because your past is your version, only a story seen through your own eyes. There are as many accounts of the same event as there are observers. Developing a knack for finding facts using truth and science provides us with the knowledge we need to understand ourselves and others in the present moment. It is not uncommon to hear someone say, even before the day begins, "I'm having a bad day. I had a terrible childhood."

Knowing how you feel can establish a firmer footing for improved emotional intelligence. Far better than the slippery slope of imagining why we feel as we do—only proving what you've believed about yourself and your existence all along.

You know what to do.

No one ever drowned in sweat.

Please visit Amazon.com to leave a review of this book.

Check out *Go Suck A Lemon: Strategies for Improving your Emotional Intelligence*. Thank you for reading!

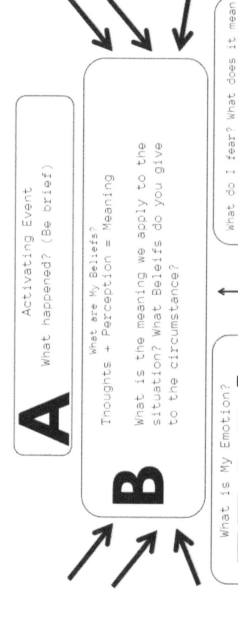

A   Activating Event
What happened? (Be brief)

What are My Beliefs?

Thoughts + Perception = Meaning

What is the meaning we apply to the
situation? What Beleifs do you give
to the circumstance?

B

What is My Emotion?

FEAR!

What do I fear? What does it mean
about me? What do I think should,
must, ought, has to, or needs to
be in order for me to be
content?

C

D   Can I prove what I tell myself at C
is true. Is it fact, truth, can it be
proved in science? What is the truth, fact,
and science of this situation? Can I be
content even if I don't get what I want?

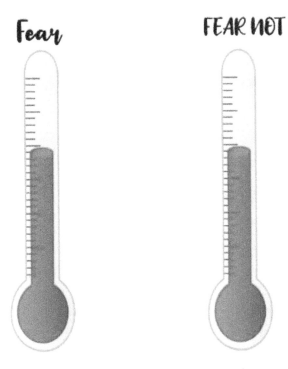

Fear

FEAR NOT

Thinking and Perception
Temperment
Genetics

Fear

FEAR NOT

Depression
Anger
Jealousy
Guilt
Grief
Frustration
Sadness

Thinking and Perception
Temperament
Genetics

Fear

Depression

Anger

Jealousy

Guilt

Grief

Frustration

Sadness

FEAR NOT

Contentment

Love

Altruism

Empathy

Collaboration

Cooperation

Joint Attention

Pointing

Curiosity

Matching/Normal

Copying

Thinking and Perception

Temperment

Genetics

Erikson's Stage Theory in its Final Version

Age	Conflict	Resolution or "Virtue"	Culmination in old age
Infancy (0-1 year)	Basic trust vs. mistrust	Hope	Appreciation of interdependence and relatedness
Early childhood (1-3 years)	Autonomy vs. shame	Will	Acceptance of the cycle of life, from integration to disintegration
Play age (3-6 years)	Initiative vs. guilt	Purpose	Humor; empathy; resilience
School age (6-12 years)	Industry vs. Inferiority	Competence	Humility; acceptance of the course of one's life and unfulfilled hopes
Adolescence (12-19 years)	Identity vs. Confusion	Fidelity	Sense of complexity of life; merging of sensory, logical and aesthetic perception
Early adulthood (20-25 years)	Intimacy vs. Isolation	Love	Sense of the complexity of relationships; value of tenderness and loving freely
Adulthood (26-64 years)	Generativity vs. stagnation	Care	Caritas, caring for others, and agape, empathy and concern
Old age (65-death)	Integrity vs. Despair	Wisdom	Existential identity; a sense of integrity strong enough to withstand physical disintegration

ABCDE Model

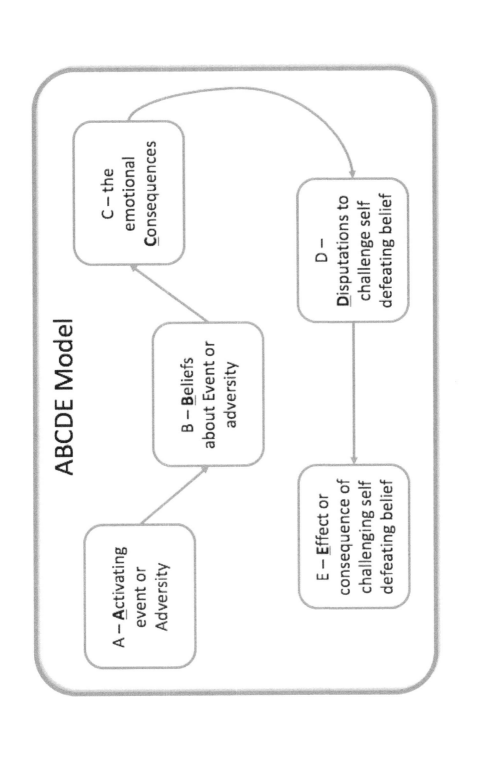

A – **A**ctivating event or Adversity

B – **B**eliefs about Event or adversity

C – the emotional **C**onsequences

D – **D**isputations to challenge self defeating belief

E – **E**ffect or consequence of challenging self defeating belief

Made in the USA
Las Vegas, NV
24 October 2023

79664139R00154